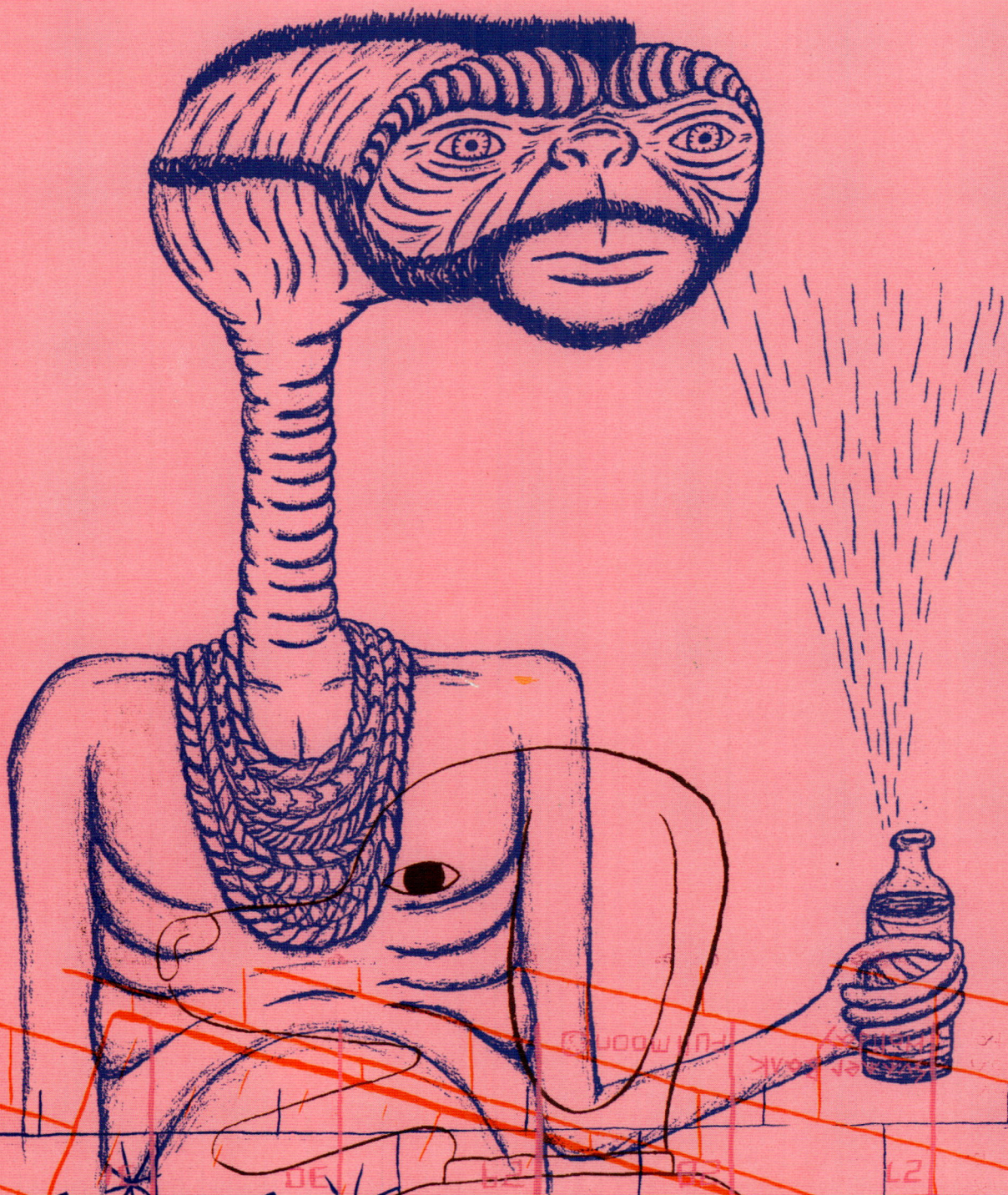

First Published in the United States of America in 2009

Gingko Press, Inc.
1321 Fifth Street
Berkeley, CA 94710, USA
Phone (510) 898-1195
email: books@gingkopress.com
www.gingkopress.com

ISBN: 978-1-58423-346-6

Printed in China

© 2009 JUXTAPOZ
www.juxtapoz.com

Produced by: R. Rock Enterprises
Design by: Justin Van Hoy / The Dutch Press
Project Manager: Z. Oxford
Writer: Kevin Thomson

Previous Page Image by Andrew Jeffrey Wright
Opposite Page Image by Jesse LeDoux

Cover Image by Paul Insect

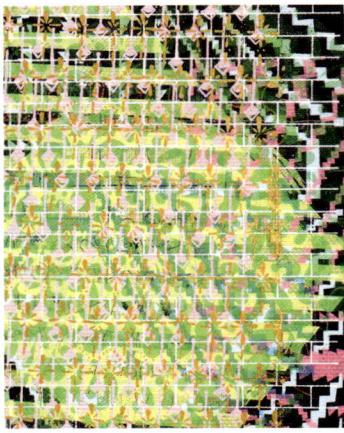

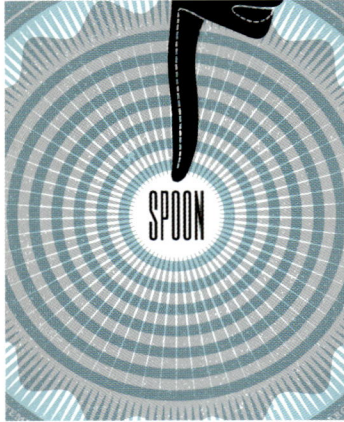

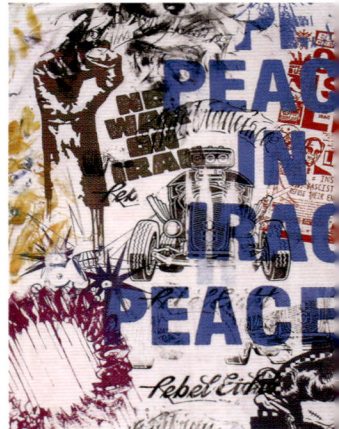

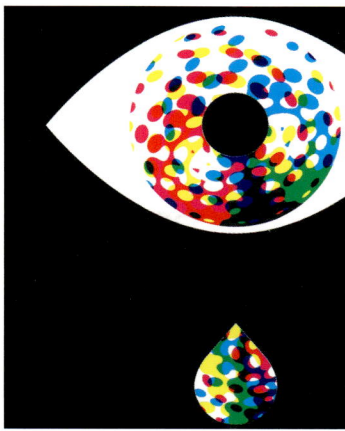

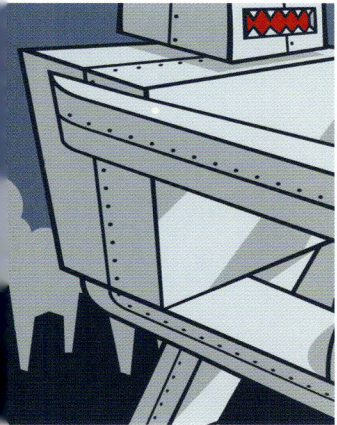

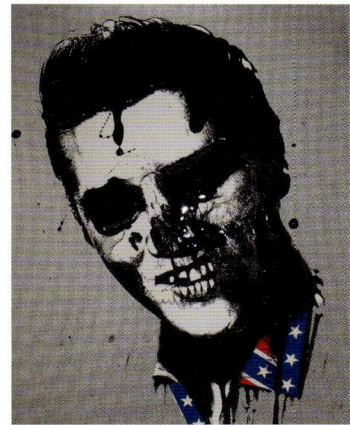
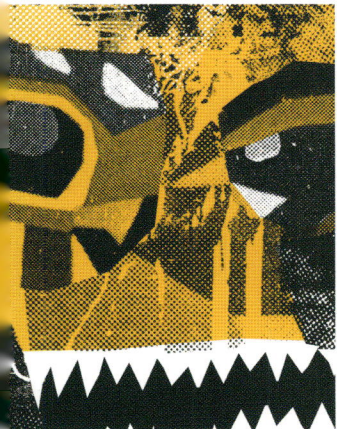

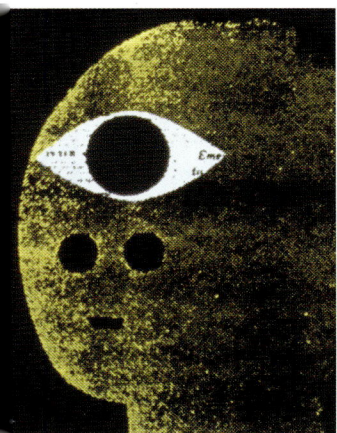

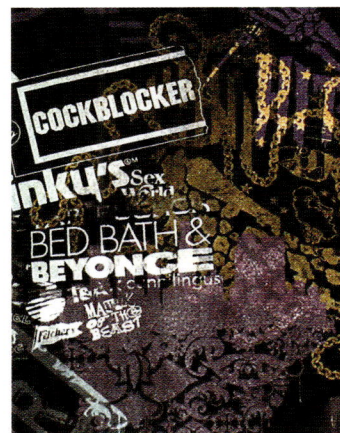

CONTENTS

INTRODUCTION

Juxtapoz Art & Culture Magazine

The third book in an ongoing series from the seminal West Coast art and culture magazine, *Juxtapoz Poster Art*, focuses on the art of screenprints. Screenprinting is the medium of the workingman's artist. It is the platform from which an artist can become world-renowned without the luxury of a big budget or the backing of a sophisticated gallery. Screenprinting is the people's art, and in the era of mass production and consumption, the handmade and precious are symbols of rebellion.

The rock poster movement evolved on the streets of San Francisco in the late 1960s. In the mid-'80s, Frank Kozik redefined what the rock poster could be with his psychedelic-meets-punk approach. Shock and juxtaposition took center stage in Kozik's images. Among those he influenced was Seattle's Art Chantry, a considerable force during the grunge movement. Much like the music itself, Chantry's posters invoked a guttural imperative built from tattered, recycled elements.

Over the years, poster art has continually progressed, with influences from comic books and the ever-so-strange style of the '80s. Along the way, a subculture of fans arose in awe of the craftsmen who perfected the artful technique of screenprinting posters.

One might claim screenprinting is making a comeback, but the truth is that screenprinting is bigger now than ever. In the past 10 years, screenprinting has ballooned in popularity and a new class of artist has emerged. These artists stepped away from the psychedelic posters of the '60s and developed their own aesthetic—incorporating everything from hand-drawn type to found objects. Their posters have become sought-after collectors' items for art and music fans alike. Featured artists include Aesthetic Apparatus, Ben Woodward, Bill McRight, Burlesque of North America, Emek, Invisible Creature, Jeff Kleinsmith, Jesse LeDoux, Little Friends of Printmaking, Paul Insect, Rocky Grimes, Seripop, Shepard Fairey, Steven Harrington, Tim Gough and more.

Imagery by Brandy Flower, Jason Munn & The Decoder Ring

AESTHETIC APPARATUS

Minneapolis design studio Aesthetic Apparatus caters to a diverse clientele—from indie band Low to corporate behemoth Burger King. They'll riff on clean, contemporary design for one project, then cut and paste punk images for another. With a solid reputation built on designing gig posters, Dan Ibarra, Mike Byzewski and newcomer Jonathan Schuster find themselves far beyond the beer-fueled confines of their first studio.

Aesthetic Apparatus lends its inspiring and interesting sensibility to everything from music magazines to science journals. Splinters of '50s and '60s design, found objects and cultural ephemera make their way into Ibarra and Byzewski's work. Since the addition of Schuster to the studio, cooperation is now a part of their process. "Before Jonathan, the two of us usually didn't collaborate too directly," Ibarra explains. "We just didn't need to. We would definitely offer up suggestions on each other's posters, but we have such a similar mind and aesthetic, there's never any real reason to collaborate, since we would've both made the same thing anyway. Jonathan's addition has actually pushed us to expand the way we both work."

Ibarra and Byzewski first met in 1998 as designers at Planet Propaganda, a design agency in Madison, Wisconsin. They moved to Minneapolis and set up AA in 2002. Today, all of their printing is done in-house, although they stopped hand pulling after "losing sensation" in their fingers. Between drinking rounds of Bell's Two Hearted Ale and "having a good laugh at the expense of anybody who's not around," the guys have taught design at Minneapolis College of Art and Design and worked on projects for clients such as Adult Swim and the Criterion Collection, and national bands such as the New Pornographers, the Hold Steady, Frank Black and local favorites STNNNG and the Deaths.

Their work has been featured in *Communication Arts*, *Creative Review*, *Print*, *Rolling Stone*, *Jane*, *ReadyMade* and Chronicle Books' rock-art bible *The Art of Modern Rock*. A collaboration with the estate of artist Jim Flora keeps Aesthetic Apparatus busy making high-end prints of Flora's work. Most recently, they are adding more illustration-based projects to their portfolio and experimenting with their ever-expanding "Doomdrips" series.

the New
Pornographers
FIRST AVENUE • OCTOBER 16, 2007 7:30PM • 18+
w/ EMMA POLLOCK & BENJY FERREE

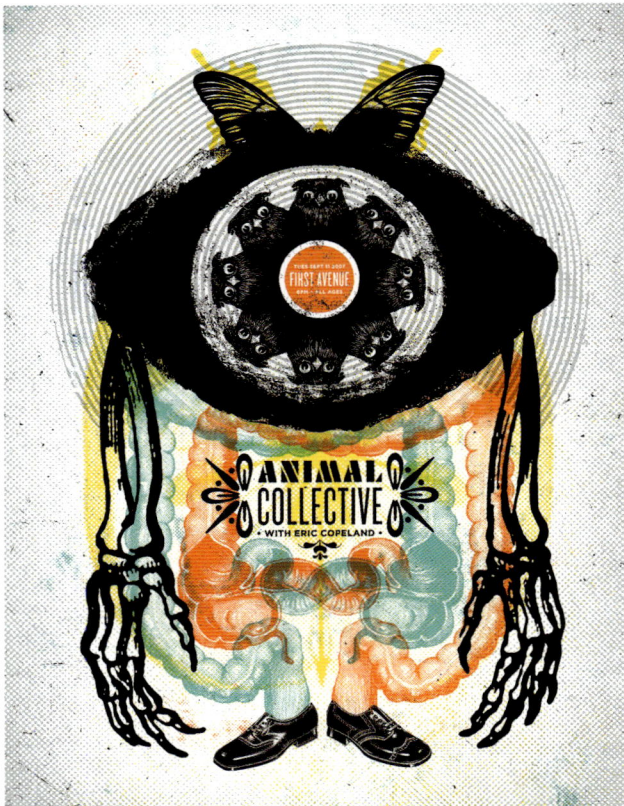

MARCH 24 WITH THE PAPER CHASE & ELUVIUM | MARCH 25 WITH ELUVIUM | THE OPERA HOUSE | TORONTO

EXPLOSIONS IN THE SKY

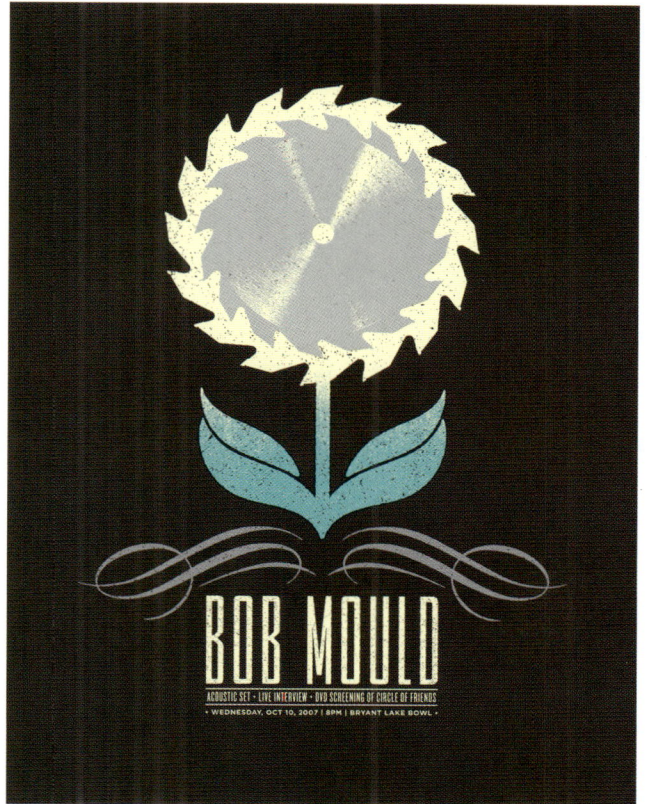

BOB MOULD

ACOUSTIC SET · LIVE INTERVIEW · DVD SCREENING OF CIRCLE OF FRIENDS
· WEDNESDAY, OCT 10, 2007 | 8PM | BRYANT LAKE BOWL ·

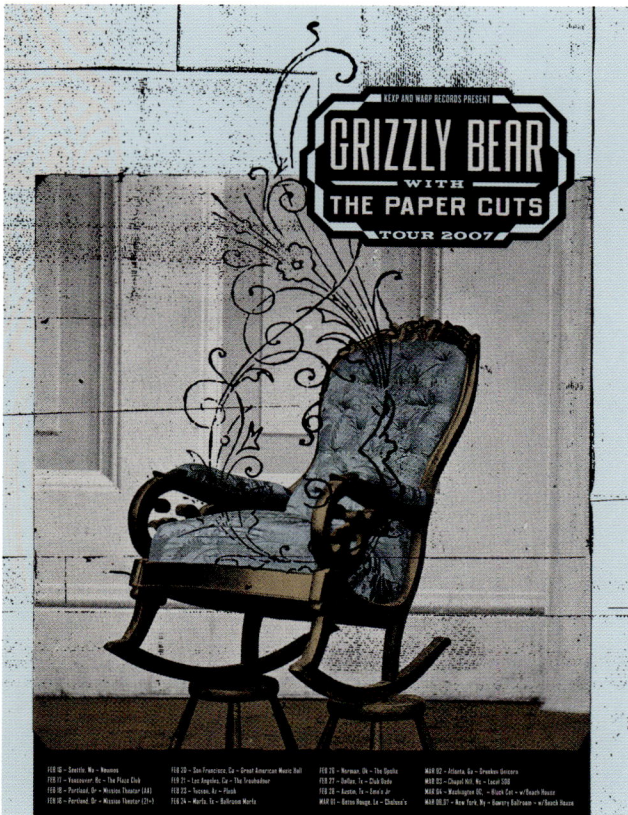

KEXP AND WARP RECORDS PRESENT

GRIZZLY BEAR
WITH
THE PAPER CUTS
TOUR 2007

SPOON

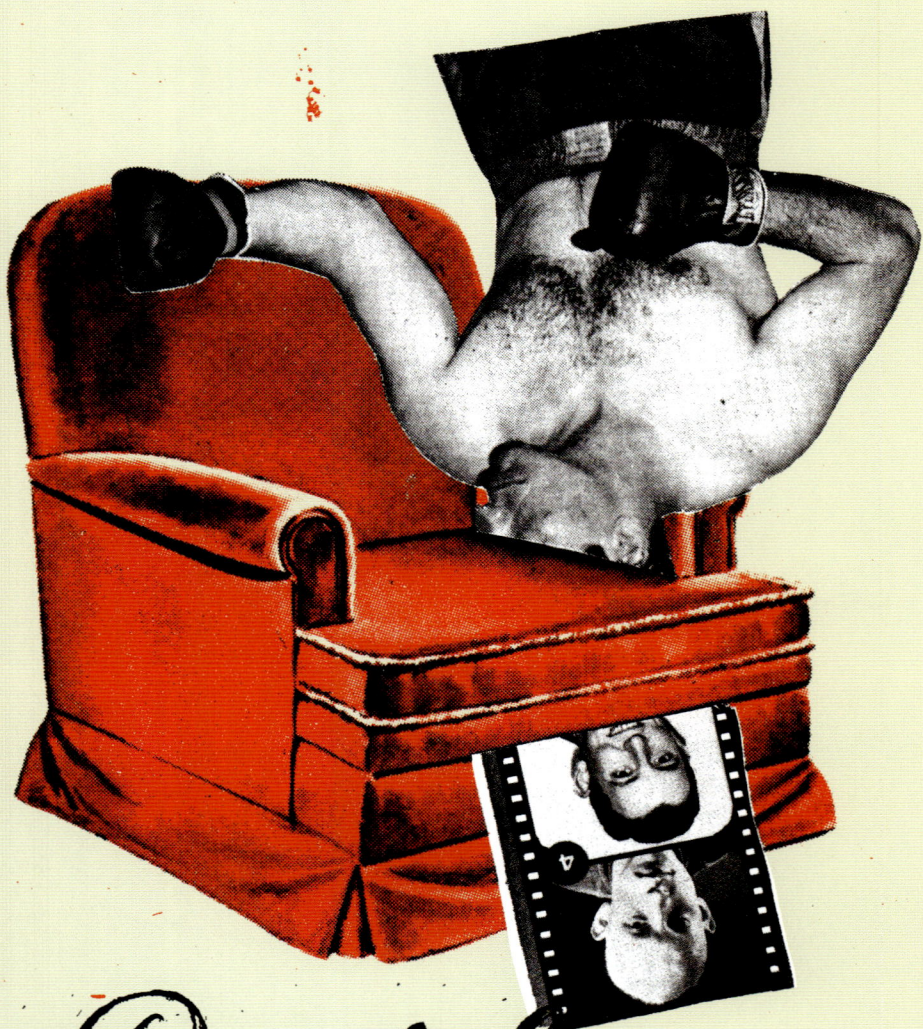

Daniel
JOHNSTON
FRIDAY, FEB 8 2:00
FIRST AVENUE P.M.
$15.00

RGG Nº 173
WWW.RICHARDGOODALLGALLERY.COM

TARGET CONCERTS

The Decemberists

CRIMSON FIRE

SEPT 25, 2007
KARLSRUHE, GERMANY
SUBSTAGE

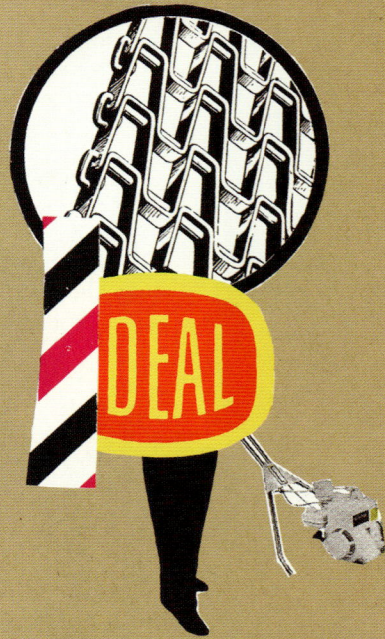

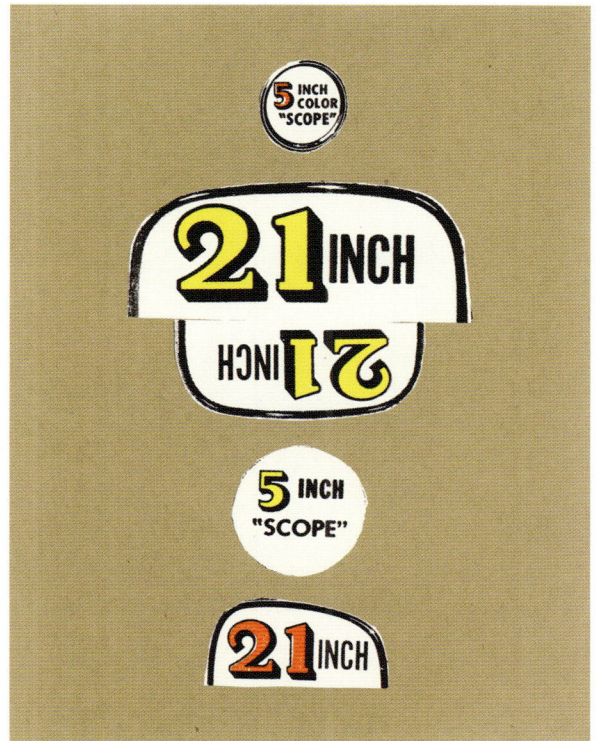

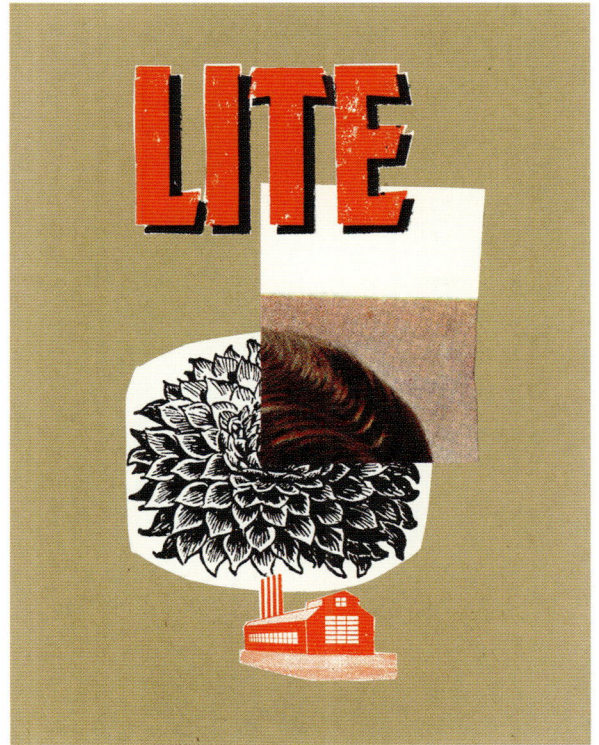

THE BIRD MACHINE

Jay Ryan learned to screenprint at Steve Walter's Screwball Press, a Chicago-based shop known for its indie-rock posters. He made his first screenprinted poster—a sketch rendered in yellow and black ink on white paper—in 1995 for a show featuring the Supersuckers, Rocket from the Crypt and the Wesley Willis Fiasco. At first, Ryan filled his portfolio with posters designed for his band, Dianogah, and friends' bands, but eventually found work with others—such as June of 44, Shellac and Fugazi—and began screenprinting full time. In 1999, he founded the Bird Machine, Inc., a poster workshop now based in Skokie, Illinois.

Ryan's work is often inhabited by playful animals, such as a bear running with scissors or a cat riding a toaster. "Play is the best way to push boundaries; find out what's possible," Ryan says. "Having fun doing my work means I wake up every day anxious to get to work. Playing with the images means I try to do something a little new with each new poster." References to

skateboarding can also be found in his work. "The action, the stretched-out full-body gesture of the skaters doing judo airs and smith grinds had a huge influence on me, and still does," he says.

A hallmark of the Bird Machine philosophy is the DIY approach, noticeable in the use of hand-drawn type. "I enjoy drawing the letterforms much more than I ever would enjoy typing them out," he says. "I can make the letters do what I want—most of the time—and in this day, with the preponderance of perfectly justified, page-layout-programmed websites, magazines and billboards we surround ourselves with, there's a certain charm to imperfect hand-drawn type. I hope others feel the same."

In 2005, Ryan compiled his favorite posters in a book titled *100 Posters/134 Squirrels*, and he is now working on a second collection.

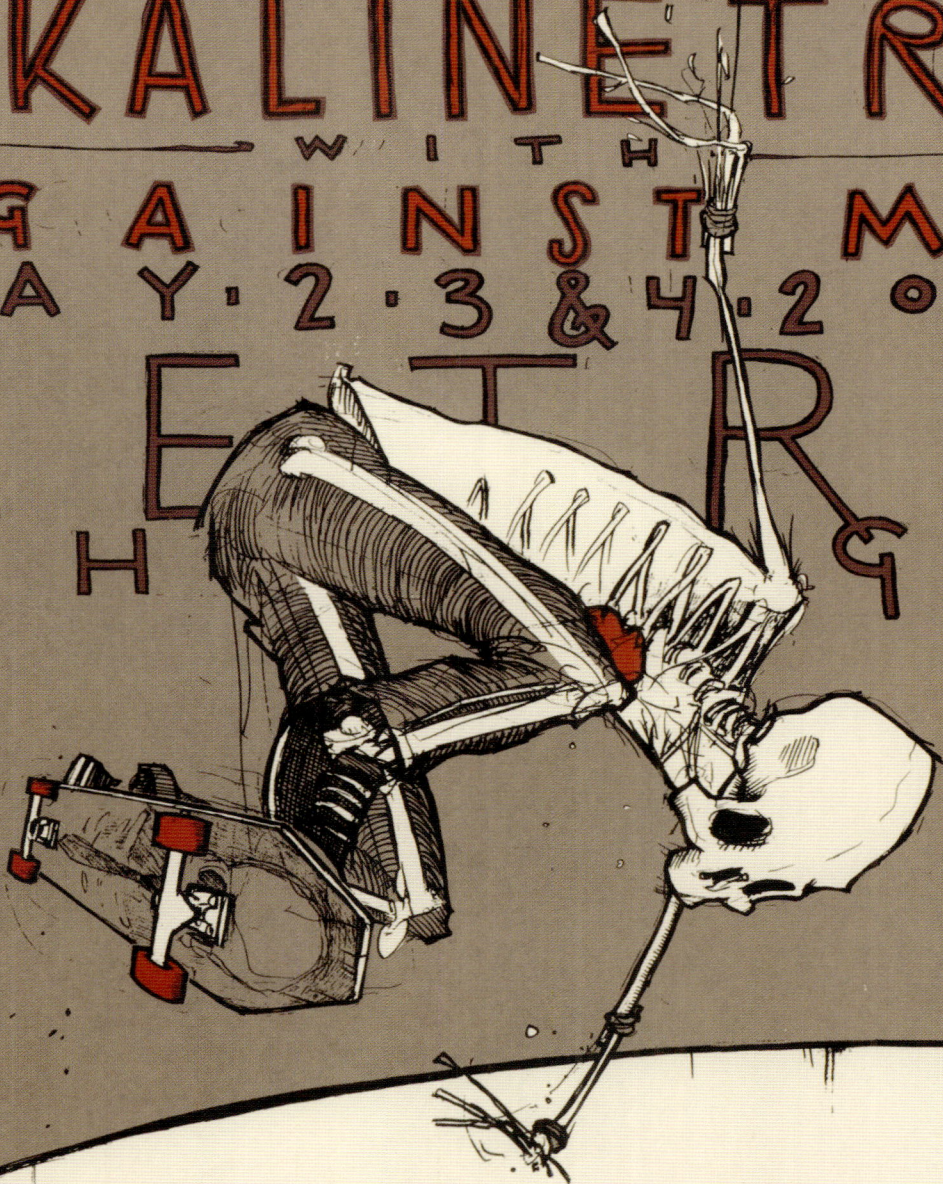

ALKALINE TRIO
WITH
AGAINST ME!
MAY·2·3&4·2006
METRO
CHICAGO

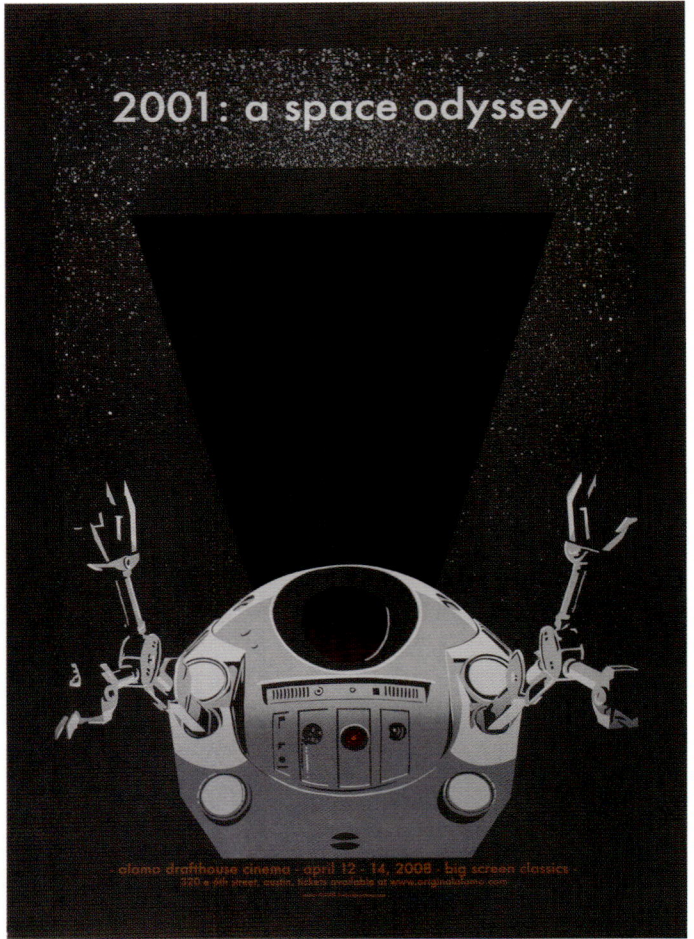

2001: a space odyssey

alamo drafthouse cinema · april 12 - 14, 2008 · big screen classics
320 e 6th street, austin. tickets available at www.originalalamo.com

DOLPHIN GHOST GENERATOR

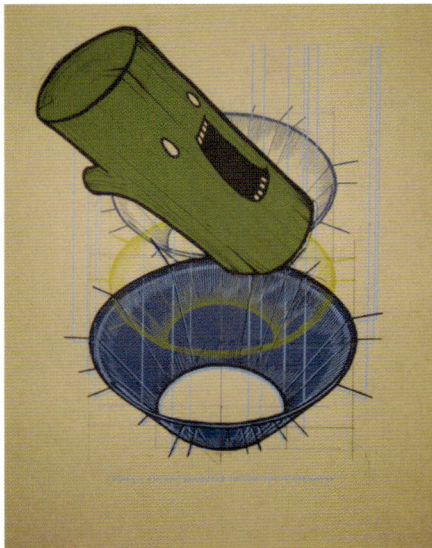

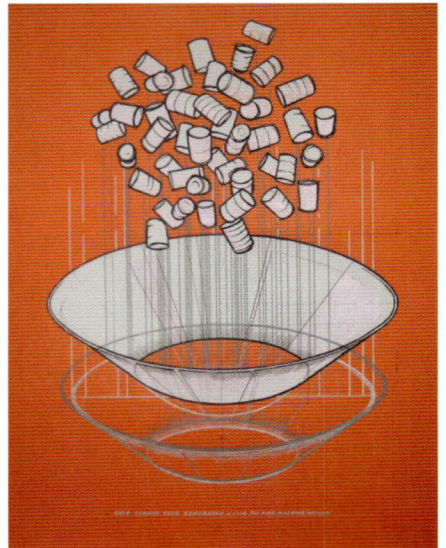

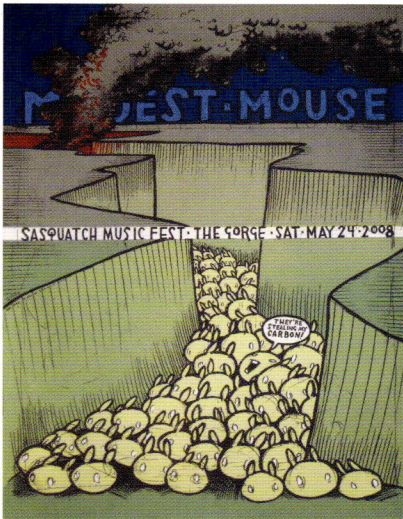

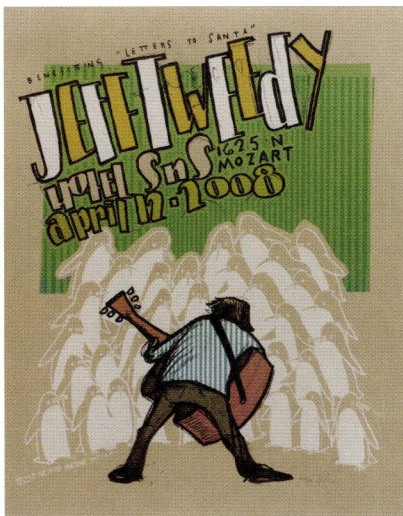

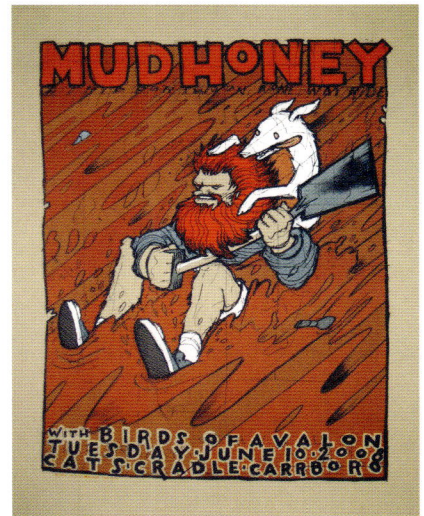

BRANDY FLOWER

Brandy Flower began screenprinting in 2001, with such newfound joy in the process that he started to throw apartment parties featuring live screenprinting. In 2005, he formed Hit+Run with Mike Crivello. The team embraced an on-the-spot assault, showing up on location to unleash inky madness on crowds. There have been more than a hundred different happenings, with a wide range of participants, including Levi's, dublab, Stones Throw Records, the Los Angeles Philharmonic, Nike, the Natural History Museum of Los Angeles, Element Skateboards and more. Each event features six unique designs, which the public gets to choose and combine in any way they want, with more adventurous attendees sometimes even pulling their own ink.

The Hit+Run phenomenon has become increasingly popular, with hopeful participants sometimes waiting in line for an hour or more. However, Flower and Crivello have not abandoned their desire to challenge systems of information exchange. Corporate logos and political figures are also exposed to the Hit+Run technique—the continuation of a project called "Mark of the Beast"—and rendered provocatively humorous.

Flower observes that the essence of the artwork is participatory, stating that "the most rewarding aspect of Hit+Run live screenprinting has been the creative interaction with the public." Flower and Crivello have emphasized the collaborative aspects of their artwork by creating a "Hit+Run Crew," an artist network consisting of other notables in street, graphic and fine art, including Cody Hudson, Maya Hayuk, Kofie, Jeff Jank, Parra, Shepard Fairey, Kevin Lyons, AMBUSCH and Restitution Press.

Flower and Crivello also focus on linking in the everyday attendant at their events. Flower notes, "Involving people in the process gives them a better understanding and deeper appreciation of the art form. I don't think many people get the opportunity to be very creative each and every day, so when the opportunity arises to make some art, they jump in headfirst! Everyone has their own aesthetics and style inside of themselves, and it has been fun to bring that out of people and collaborate with them. Most people walk away from a Hit+Run event with a true sense of individual expression—and their new favorite shirt! Someone once said we re-invented the concert T-shirt, and I think it's true. There's a revolution happening, and we're on the front line."

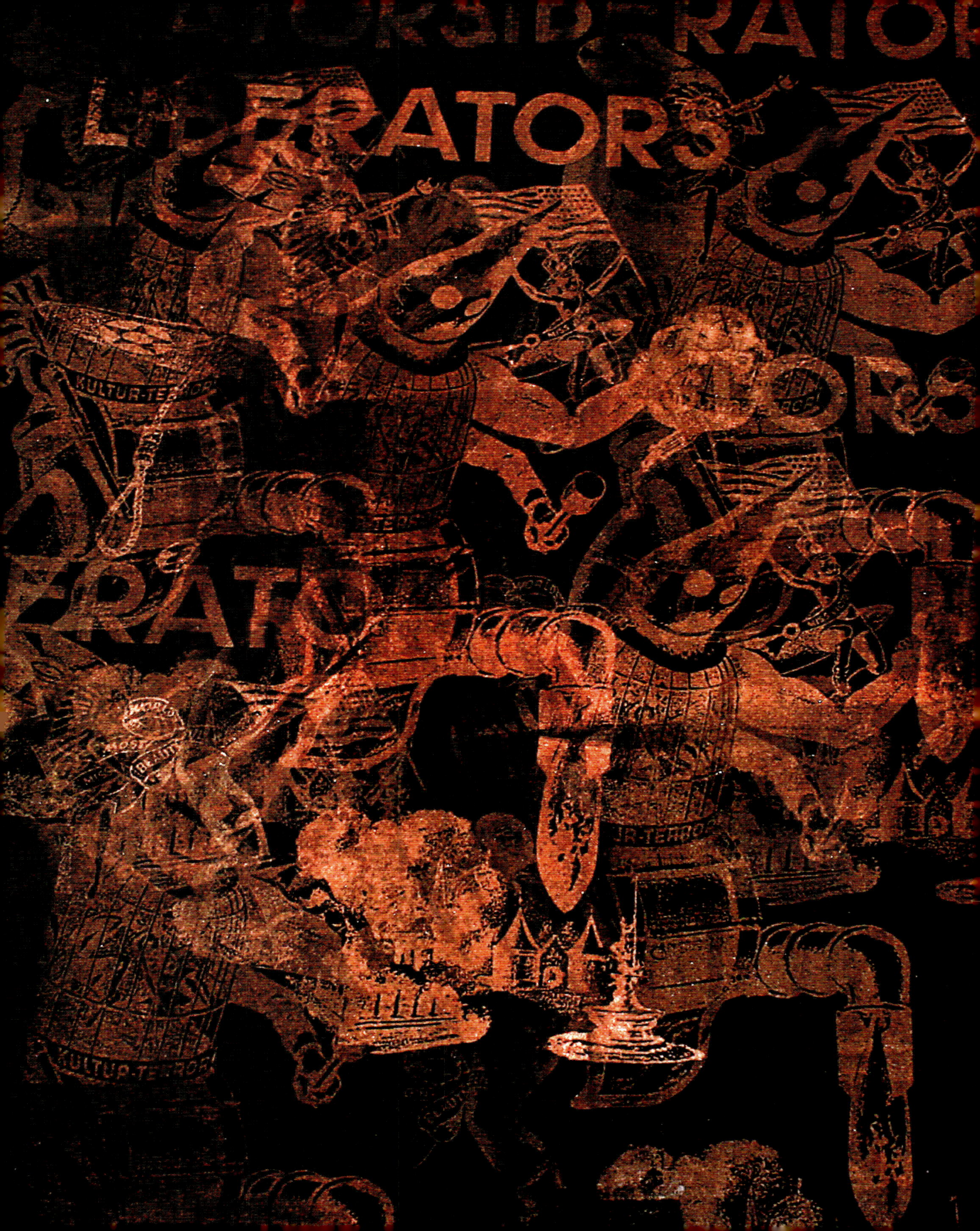
KULTUR-TERROR

GONUTS
COCKBLOCKER
Cunts
FREAK
JACK N' DANNY
FUCK
Cheaters
EVILS
Sex World
STAR FUCKER
BED BATH &
BEYONCE
T&A
cunnilingus
Still-on drugs
YAYO!
D.A.R.E.
Los Angeles Crimes
Vain Bitch
LIBERATORS
ENOUGH
Cheaters
Newsweek
Sparkalot
Dope
cotton mouth
POWER TRIPPERS
Shellea
BOMBING
LAND O FAKES
IMPEACH BUSH
EVILS
osul
TIKRIT
Shrapnel
TALIBAN
Coke diet
KRAK
LIBERAT
IBERATO
OIL of IRAQ
STOP WARS
BOMBING
COCKBLOCKER
STAR FUCK
BED BAT
BEYONCE
Vain Bitch
Disillusioned
Sparkalot
Cocaine
Dope
cotton mouth
Pillpopper
D.A.R.E.
DRUGS ARE REALLY EXPENSIVE
Coke diet
MAUI Wowee
Highagain
ACID
DRUG WARS
Kronik
Marijuana
Shellea
Cheaters
Newsweek
POWER TRIPPERS
IMPEACH BUSH
PAC BOWL
STONY
BOMBING
BOMB

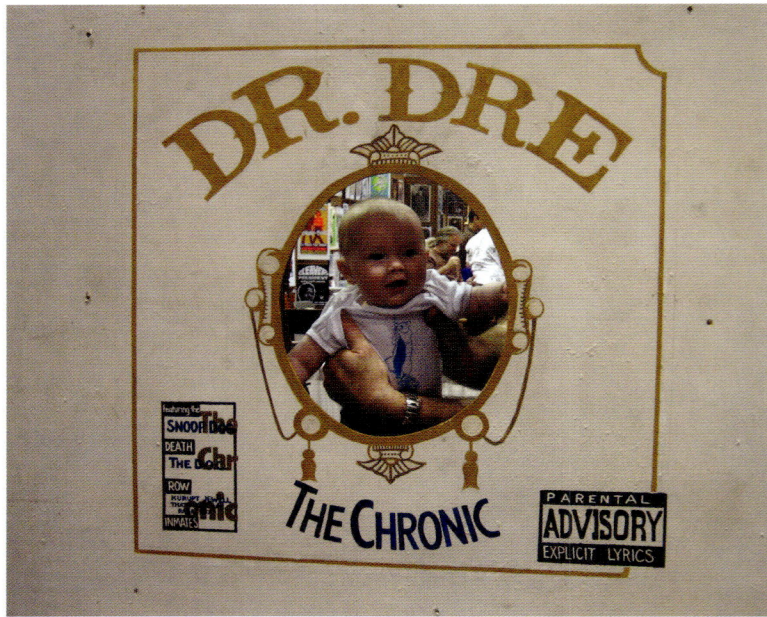

BURLESQUE DESIGN

Burlesque of North America is a Minneapolis-based design and screenprinting studio consisting of five who create (Wes Winship, Mike Davis, Aaron Horkey, Todd Bratrud and George Thompson) and a production staff comprised of Bjorn Christianson, Ben Lafond, Jodi Milbert and Peter Bekke. "The whole process from start to finish is a huge collaboration between all of the different staff members," Davis explains.

With so much give and take at the shop, it is difficult to pinpoint Burlesque's style. "There is no all-encompassing aesthetic or look to what we do, since all of the artists have their own styles they bring to the table," Davis says. "Perhaps our aesthetic is that mish-mosh of mismatched aesthetics."

Burlesque has designed countless music-related items for clients such as Arcade Fire, Converge, Rhymesayers, Boris, Stones Throw Records, Isis,

Andrew Bird and the Bonnaroo Festival. In 2008, they organized a party during the SXSW music festival and decided to produce a 12-inch single. "The DJs spinning our opening night submitted remixes they had done, so we compiled them and pressed them onto vinyl, then designed and screenprinted the packaging ourselves for that special Burlesque touch," Davis says. "The record has been a great success, and we're planning to put out more releases. It's a great extension of our poster printing and our love of music." Burlesque's label is aptly titled BRLSQOTHEQUE.

Burlesque also curates a gallery space, creates stickers by the sack, designs skateboard decks and celebrates Dre Day. When asked about Burlesque's ultimate goal, Davis answers, "To always look forward to coming to work in the morning. We all love what we do, and as long as we can continue to love what we do, then we'll be happy, I suppose."

SATURDAY MAY 29TH 2004 8PM   TRIPLE ROCK   MINNEAPOLIS MINNESOTA   21&UP $10

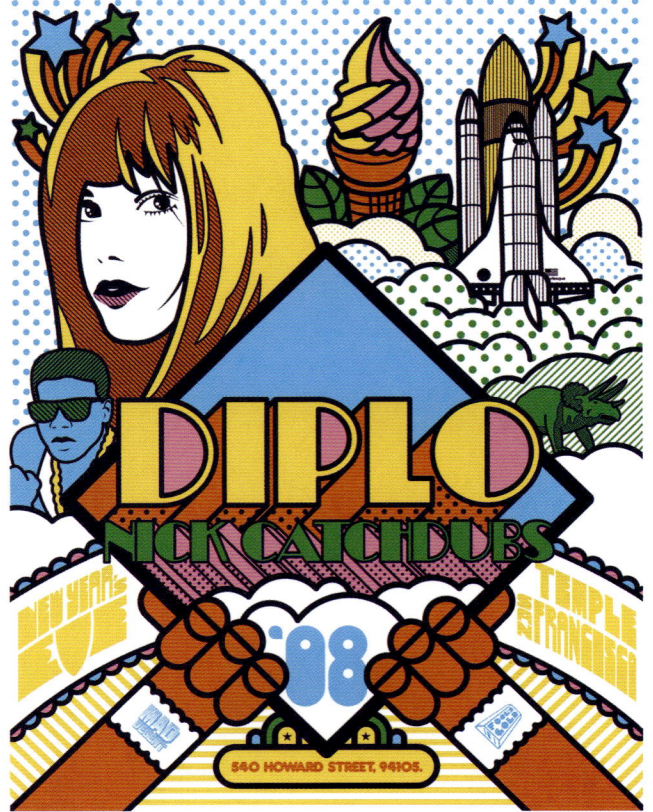

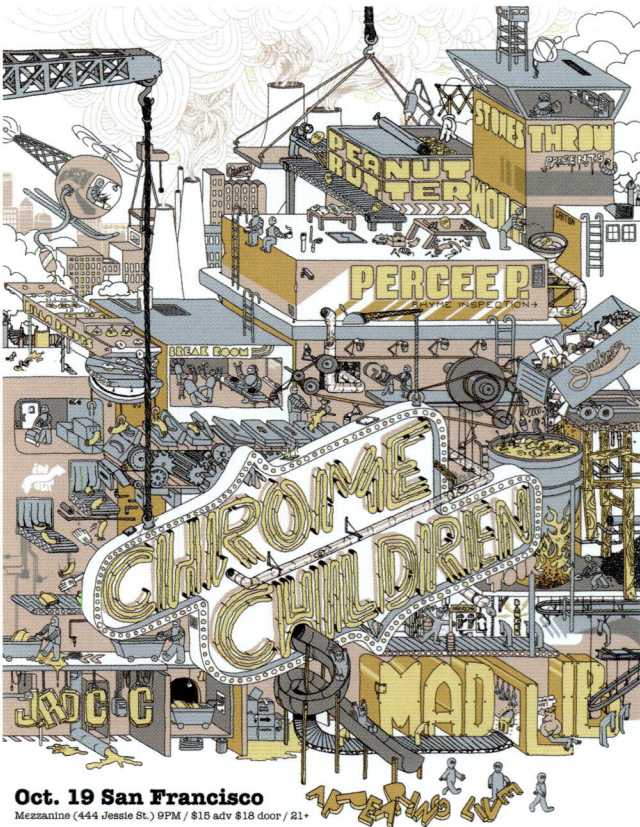

Oct. 19 San Francisco
Mezzanine (444 Jessie St.) 9PM / $15 adv $18 door / 21+

THE DECODER RING
DESIGN CONCERN

Located in Austin, Texas, the Decoder Ring Design Concern is made up of Christian Helms, Geoff Peveto and Paul Fucik. All three work on design, with Helms leading the way and Fucik and Peveto handling the screenprinting. "There is a lot of overlap, however," Peveto says. "The experience Paul and I bring from screenprinting really partners with Christian's understanding of design and vice versa."

The Decoder Ring enjoys experimenting, such as trying out alternative printing techniques or odd substrates; they have printed projects on everything from player-piano rolls to 40-ounce paper bags. "The disasters just serve to fuel solutions down the road," Peveto says. "The metallic ink, varnishes, wax or coffee that didn't work today will be the key to a unique execution next month."

Each member of the Decoder Ring brings his own styles, interests and specialties to the table. "We have enough commonalities to relate to each other, but what we really enjoy are our differences," says Peveto. "We each work in different ways and have varying criteria for a successful solution. That means lots of debate and the opportunity to be challenged every day. I use a lot of photography, and Christian tends to illustrate. Paul illustrates as well, and uses a lot of found art on top of that."

The Decoder Ring fine-art print series is a collaboration between the Decoder Ring and various artists, including Gary Baseman, Dalek and Tara McPherson. Decoder Ring brings the artists to Austin to create original artwork that is then translated into a multi-layered serigraph. On the website, an interactive feature allows the viewer to see each step of the printmaking process.

In 2008, the Decoder Ring went green, using only water or soy-based printing products and post-consumer paper.

"The Good times are Killing me".
VALENTINE'S EVENING WITH MODEST MOUSE AT THE GROVE OF ANAHEIM IN SUNNY CALIFORNIA
THIS IMMACULATE MESS DESIGNED WITH LOVE BY XIAN AT THEDECODERRING.COM

SPOON AUSTRALIA

CANBERRA WED. 14
BRISBANE THUR. 15
ADELAIDE SAT. 10
PERTH SUN. 11
SYDNEY FRI. 16
NEWCASTLE SAT. 17
MELBOURNE THUR. 08 FRI. 09
SEPTEMBER TOUR
2005

POSTER DESIGN BY THEDECODERRING.COM

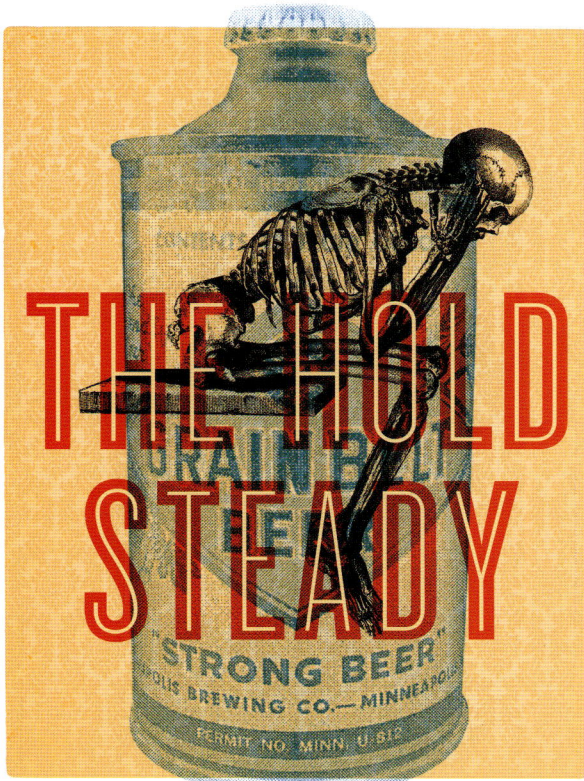

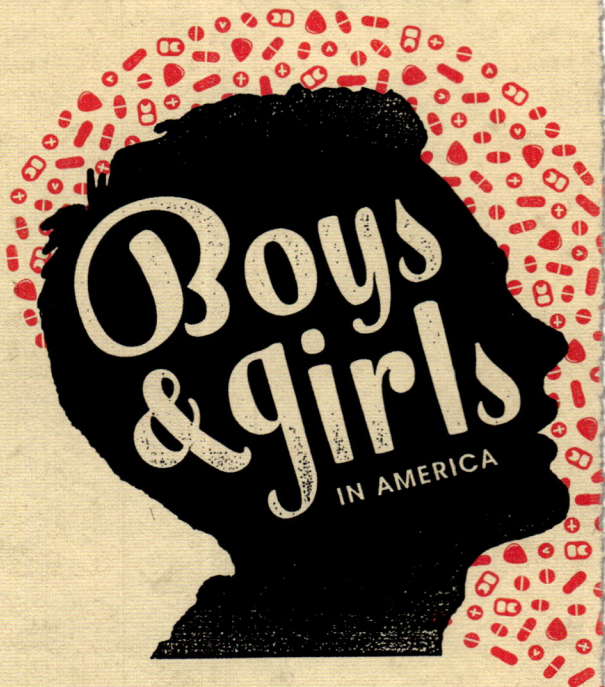

February Fifth and Sixth at Soma

"and you wound up on an island of shells and bones" poster by the decoder ring .com | PF   # _____ of 425

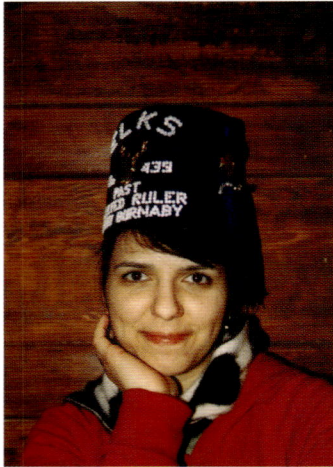

DORA DRIMALAS

Dora Drimalas' clean style references Swiss design and contemporary to midcentury modern sensibilities, lending itself to the silkscreen medium. The tactile qualities of silkscreening highlight the organic, handmade feel of Drimalas' artwork while keeping her stylistic intent intact, at home on posters as well as T-shirts. Her collaborations with her husband, Brian Flynn, have found a venue in the form of comfy pillows, which the couple sells through their company, Hybrid-Home.

In Drimalas' silkscreens, black-and-white images of playful creatures, bicycles in love, and two human forms literally connected by heartstrings burst out from vibrant, colorful backgrounds. Drimalas' work embraces a history of iconography, with images floating mid-space in the silkscreens. Contrasts are evident—the vast rectangular expanse of the single background color contrasts with the organic, circular shapes of owls, bicycle wheels and flowers. In this way, Drimalas plays with negative and positive space. Black and white also contrast within image foregrounds, with two owls in one image forming the color inverse of each other. Within the same image, a pristine bloom contrasts with a faded flower dropping its petals to the ground in the first stages of decay.

Drimalas also creates logos, retail environments, identities and branding with her husband, under the name Hybrid Design. Together they have worked for Nike, Hypebeast, Super7 and Unframed. She has also created a series of toys with her husband and five other artists, called the Neo-Kaiju series, in which they individually invented a new interpretation of a classic Japanese monster accompanied by a new companion monster for each.

A native of Athens, Georgia, Drimalas was raised in Texas and now resides in San Francisco, California, though she and her work have been around the world.

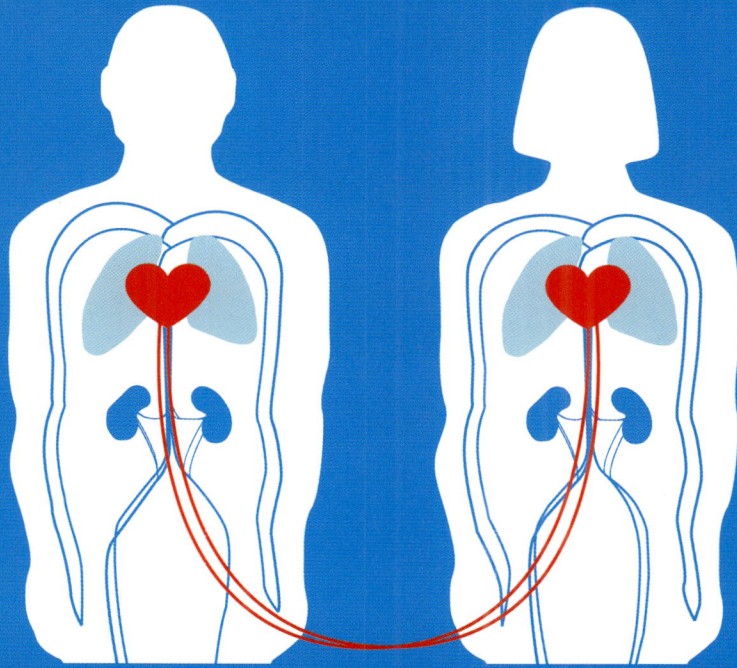

EMEK

Emek is the moniker chosen by a man bent on a creative life expressed through the power of his drafting skills and screenprinting. Born as the eldest in a family of five artists, Emek was influenced by the art, music and socially conscious 1960s attitude of his parents. "I fell in love with the limited-edition prints that I saw being handmade and yet 'mass produced' in my dad's art studio," he says.

Poster art is his chosen medium because he appreciates the "flexibility." Emek continues, "Because the bands generally give me total creative freedom, I am allowed to dip into the recesses of my imagination and see what spills out onto the page."

For his poster "High on Fire," a horizontal print featuring a lit match, Emek actually hand-burned the entire edition. "I wanted to do something that called into question the impermanence of rock posters as an art form," he says. "Their origin is that they were designed to be seen in public spaces and grab one's attention. A lot of work went into making them, but maybe next week they'll be torn down and replaced by something else. And as a paper artifact, a carelessly tossed match and it's all just a memory anyways."

Emek has also been known to cut, scratch, sculpt, cast, cook, weave and emboss his posters. "I want to stretch the poster art form," he says, "give dimension to a medium that has been traditionally flat." For example, his Flaming Lips "Modern Man as a Fossil" poster is a limited-edition resin sculpture, and his Queens of the Stone Age poster features a hand-cast working plastic spinner. "I do it all myself," he says. "From concept to sculpting to making the mold, mixing the chemicals, pouring the resins, sanding, painting, signing—in my own studio, which I built. Each piece is very personal, very hands on. Funny thing is that I work just as hard on making the silkscreens, but people appreciate the labor when it's 3-D."

Emek's work has won many awards and is coveted by collectors worldwide. He has been featured in several books, interviewed by magazines of all genres, and is on permanent display in Hard Rock Cafes all over the world.

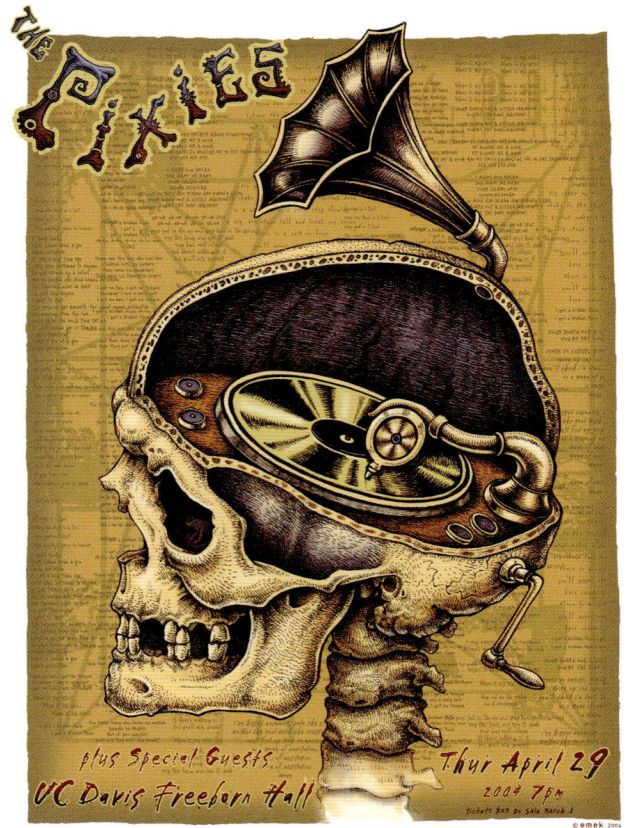

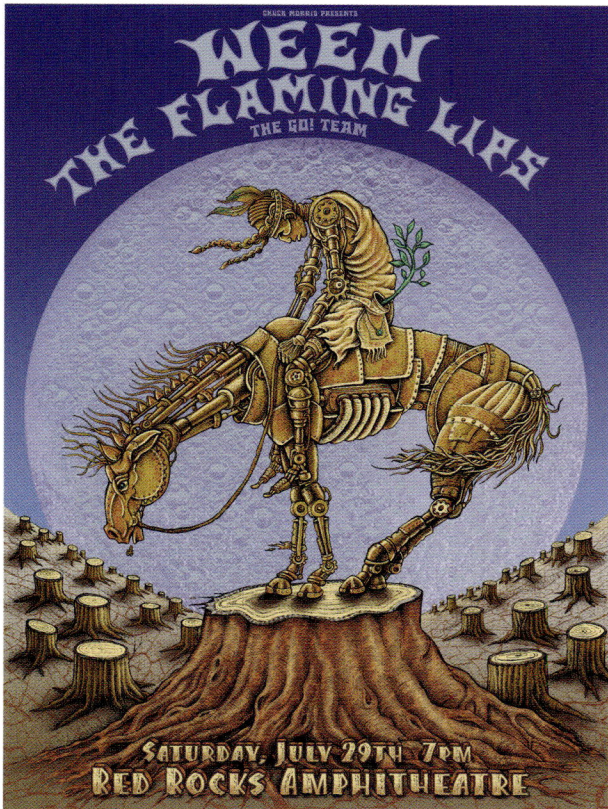

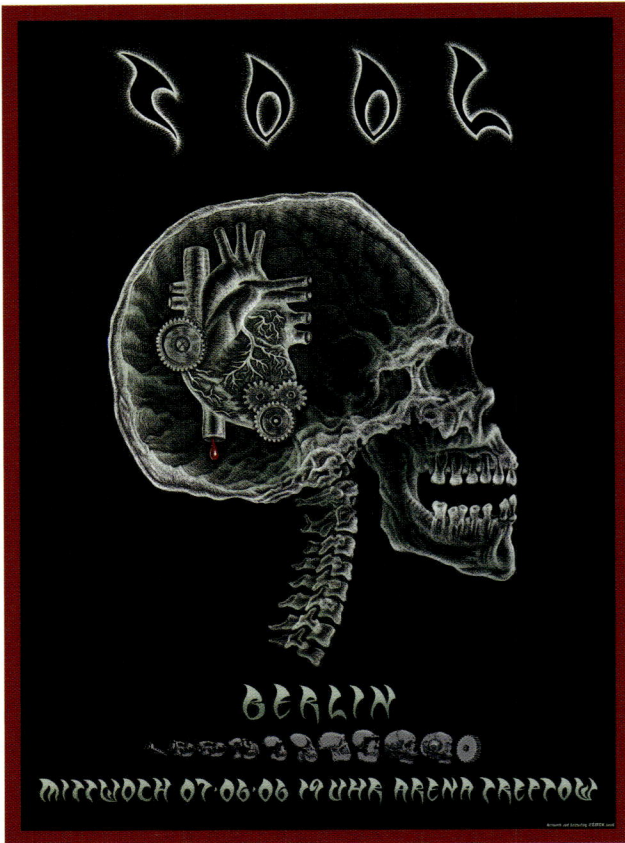

THE DECEMBERISTS

WEDNESDAY 21ST FEB. 287 WITH LAVENDER DIAMOND
PARADISO ◆ AMSTERDAM NETHERLANDS

RGG Nr.151 www.richardgoodallgallery.com   www.decemberists.com   special 11 color silkscreen ©EMEK.net 2007

50

GOLDENVOICE PRESENTS IN INDIO

COACHELLA

MARCH 27 28 29 2007
EMPIRE POLO FIELD

QUEENS OF THE STONE AGE

DETROIT
ST. ANDREWS HALL 4.30.5

July 18-21, 2007 10,000 LAKES FESTIVAL DETROIT LAKES, MN

BOB WEIR & RATDOG. THE STRING CHEESE INCIDENT. UMPHREY'S McGEE. MOE.. GOV'T MULE. THE TRAGICALLY HIP. KELLER WILLIAMS. ZAPPA PLAYS ZAPPA. THE DISCO BISCUITS. GALACTIC. THE DEREK TRUCKS BAND. PARTICLE AND OVER 50 MORE BANDS

SHEPARD FAIREY

Shepard Fairey started the ubiquitous "Andre the Giant Has a Posse" project in 1989, while attending the Rhode Island School of Design. The street-level experiment started with stickers and posters—featuring a portrait of Andre the Giant and the word "obey" in bold letters—pasted on the sides of local buildings and electricity boxes.

"The reason I got into screenprinting was because there was the ability to make multiples and your work can be in a lot of places at once," Fairey says. "I see it as a medium that is power to the people; it's not expensive to make or buy, and yet they are unique pieces of art."

As his Obey Giant campaign virally grew into a global phenomenon recognized around the world, Fairey's work expanded in provocative directions. Continuing to use a screenprinting sensibility and the word "obey," he balanced presentation with message, appropriating political propaganda and spinning it on its head, which resulted in beautiful art that critiqued government, capitalism and mass media.

Fairey founded the design firm Studio Number One (SNO) in 2003. SNO offers a wide range of design services to high-profile corporate clients. Fairey also provides his services to favorite causes, such as a recent poster designed in support of pet adoption. In 2008, he created an iconic image endorsing then-presidential-candidate Barack Obama. In a video interview, Fairey told *Time* magazine, "It may be the defining image of my career, of my life."

Fairey's art has been displayed at numerous museums around the world, including The Smithsonian and the Victoria and Albert Museum, and in 2005 he was the artist in residence at Honolulu's Contemporary Museum. Most recently, Boston's Institute of Contemporary Art exhibited a major 20-year retrospective of his work.

These SUNSETS ARE TO DIE FOR!

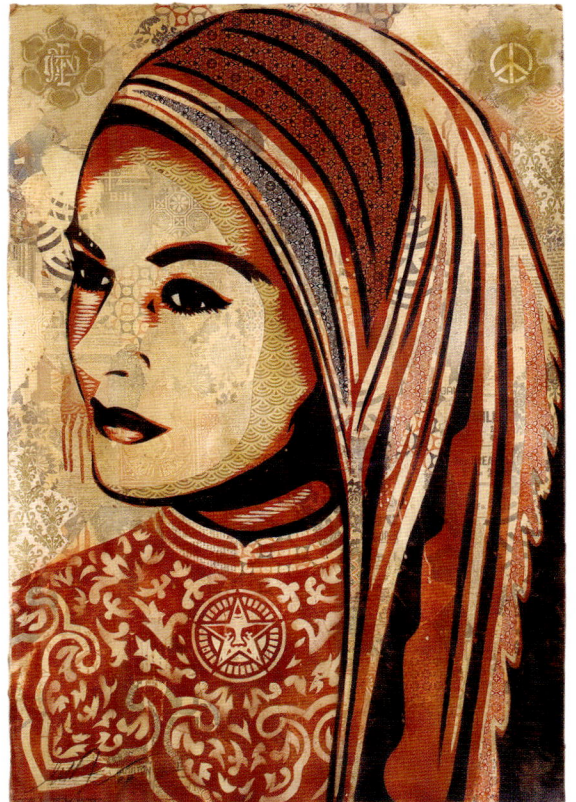

PEACE

POWER & EQUALITY

Greetings FROM IRAQ

"ENJOY A CHEAP HOLIDAY IN OTHER PEOPLE'S MISERY"

JUSTIN FINES

Justin Fines grew up in the suburbs of Detroit, where he started out in the arts by making fliers for bands and parties. In a blog for the show "Joyful Bewilderment," Fines' work is described as "the golden tint of suburban childhood nostalgia blended with the influence of the hulking abandoned factories and mansions of the Motor City. This combination creates a graphic language that balances between hope and cynicism."

Now living in Brooklyn, and working under the moniker DEMO, Fines still indulges in that language. His brightly colored work brings to mind the old-timey illustrations of children's author Richard Scarry combined with a contemporary, street-savvy aesthetic.

Fines' work has appeared on Zoo York skate decks and hoodies, Gas T-shirts, Burton snowboards, and as animations for the kids' show *Yo Gabba Gabba!* on Nick Jr. Upcoming works from DEMO include a line of snowboards for Rome SDS, a bag for CSC and Incase, and a bunch of new silkscreen prints.

His innovative designs and typography have earned awards from the Type Directors Club Annual, Print Magazine Regional Design Annual and Communication Arts Design Annual, and his art has been exhibited in galleries around the world, from London to Los Angeles.

Fines is also a member of the design collective Rad Mountain, which includes Damien Correll, Wyeth Hansen, Garret Morin and Ryan Waller. Recently, the Mountain illustrated an entire issue of *Swindle*, injecting color and warmth into stories on such serious topics as psychological operations and MS-13.

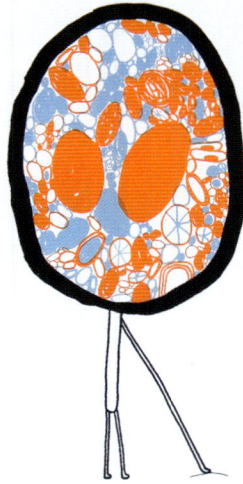

BRIAN FLYNN

San Francisco-based artist and designer Brian Flynn is a self-confessed nerd. Brought up on a steady diet of comic books, science fiction, baseball cards, monsters and robots, he retreated into the dark corners of childhood, until discovering the illicit thrills of skateboarding, taking a headfirst dive into punk and hardcore. With these extremes as his guideposts, Flynn has managed to merge his obsessions and comment about his own life experiences in graphically simple and understandable ways.

From the late '80s through the mid '90s, Flynn's fliers were strictly photocopied—at first by necessity but later as a reaction against the new silkscreened rock poster movement.

Along the way, his work was featured in several poster shows and a touring music-art exhibition, ironically recognized by *Communication Arts* magazine, where his work hung next to the silkscreens to which he was opposed. In staying loyal to the one-color photocopier, Flynn's style became more and more graphic, leading to easier recognition and reproduction. It was only later, after no longer making band fliers on a regular basis and creating artwork purely for himself, that Flynn began to use the silkscreen as a means to an end for production, but not as part of a movement.

At this point, Flynn turned again to his personal experiences and began making silkscreens that documented life's trajectory through his eyes: Rorschach tests made up of spaceship, monster or robot silhouettes from the history of science fiction; ghosts rendered as "visible innards;" maps and cross-sections of secret hideouts and underground labyrinths. Collections of heavy metal mascots, punk rock iconography and fictionalized monsters also began to surface in his work.

After a five-year stint at Nike's Brand Design in Portland, Flynn moved to San Francisco and launched his own graphic design studio, Hybrid Design, in 2000. Flynn still works closely with Nike, as well as with Apple, Sony, Converse, W Hotels, Real, Spitfire, Upper Playground, and he helped redesign *Juxtapoz* magazine in 2007.

In 2001, Flynn launched *Super7* magazine, which has since grown into a book, clothing line, retail store and toy manufacturer. Many of the toys are creatures and characters of his own design, bringing his childhood obsession full circle.

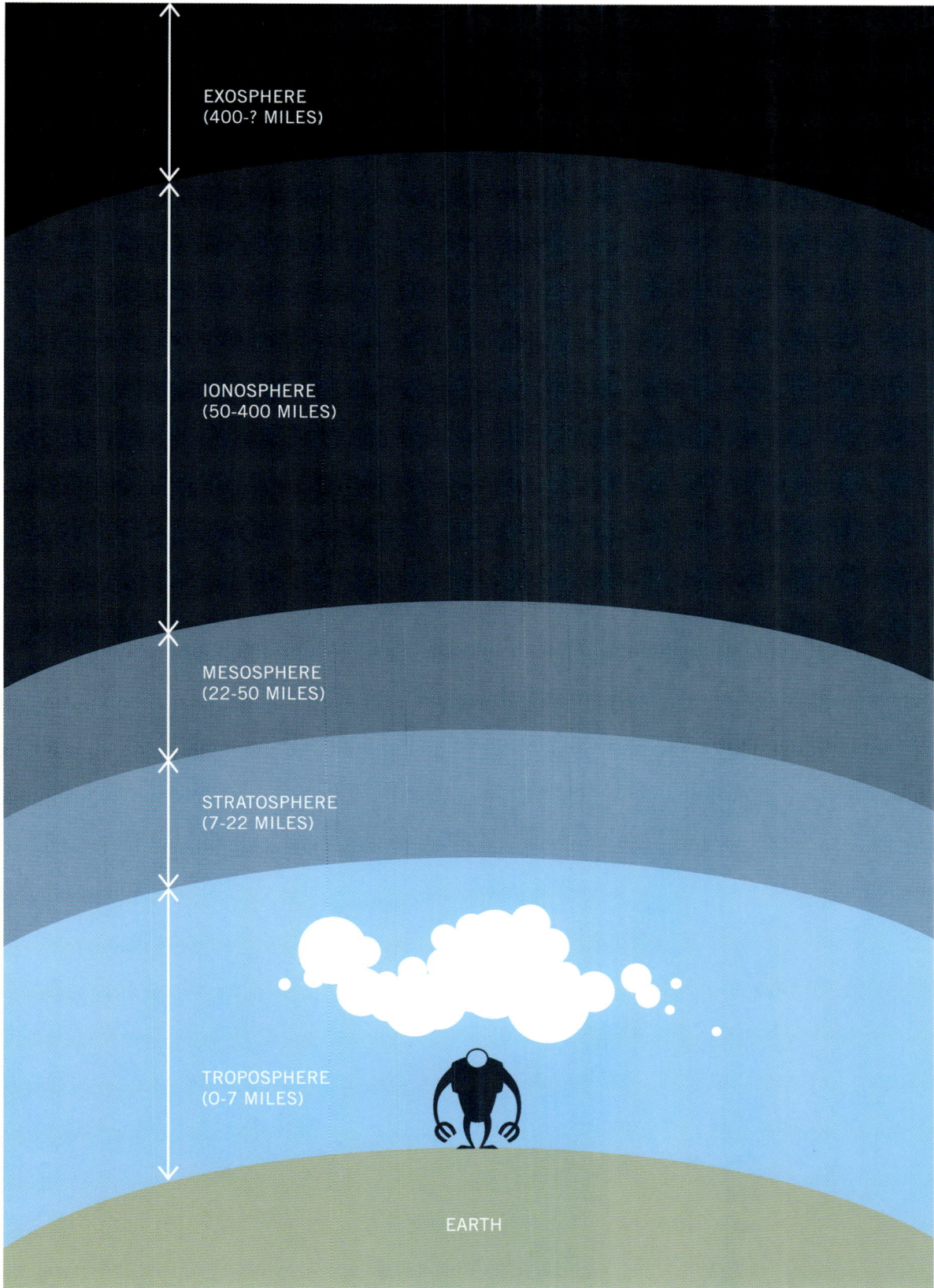

EXOSPHERE
(400-? MILES)

IONOSPHERE
(50-400 MILES)

MESOSPHERE
(22-50 MILES)

STRATOSPHERE
(7-22 MILES)

TROPOSPHERE
(0-7 MILES)

EARTH

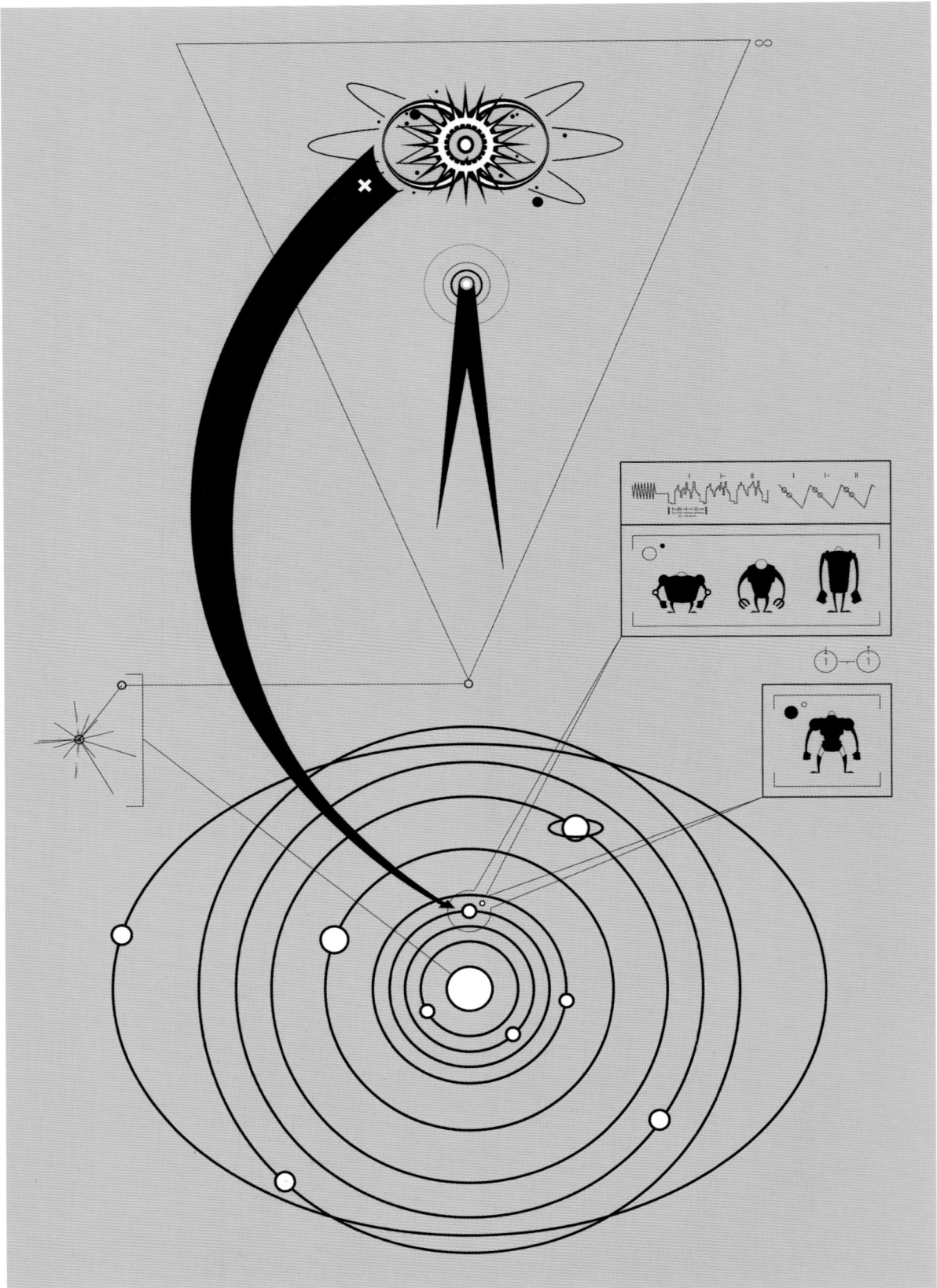

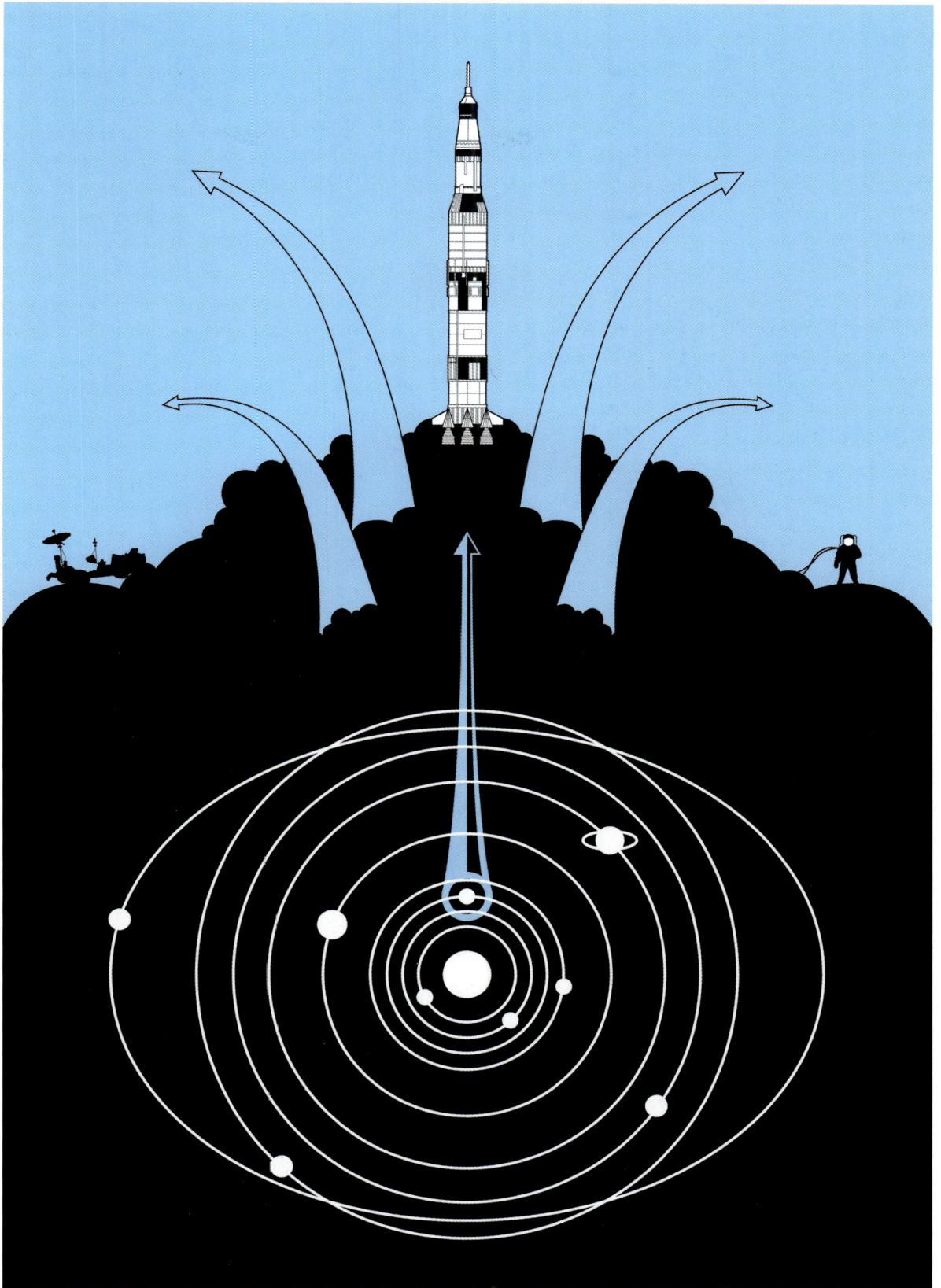

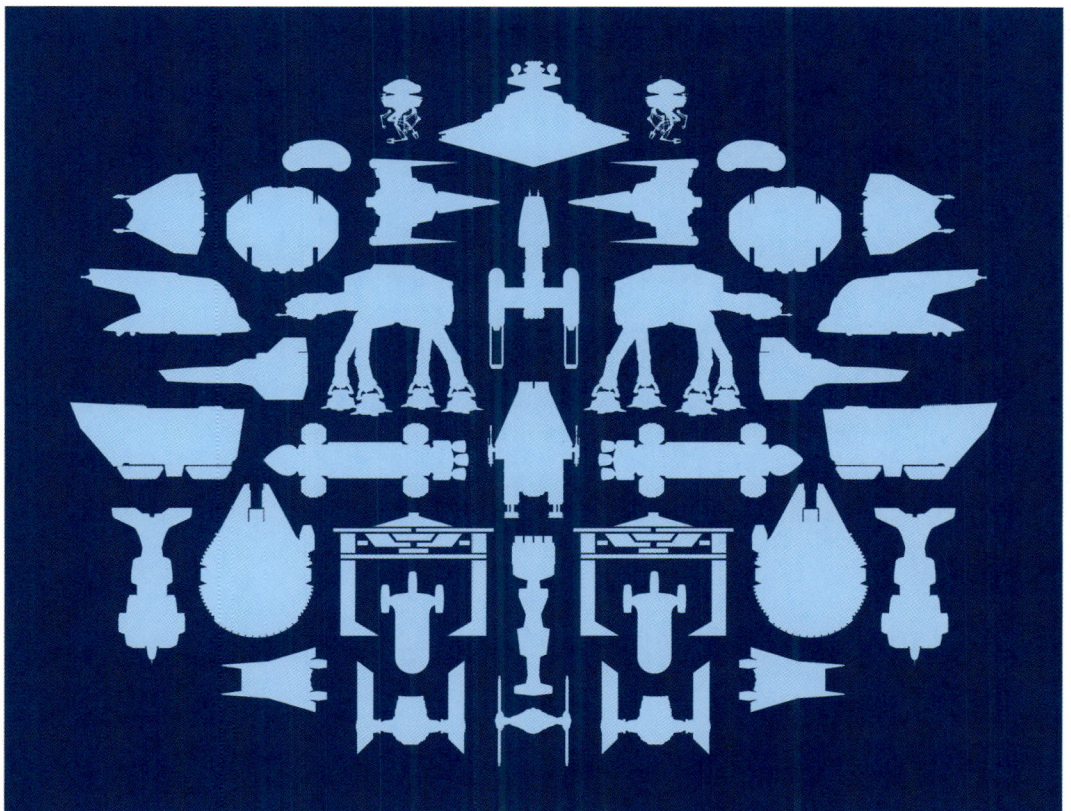

TIM GOUGH

Using limited color and basic iconography, Philly-based artist Tim Gough has created a bold, unmistakable style that he describes as "messy but simple." Gough continues, "I think something is always askew—either technique or content. The reason I like using screenprinting, photocopiers and a brush is that they all can be unpredictable; the imperfections give a nice human touch, especially now, when so much work is computer generated." Gough's work has an almost vintage feel, citing 1960s movie posters, album covers and book jackets.

Gough graduated with a degree in graphic design, but soon tired of laying out "crappy fliers and sitting in front of the computer all day. I started screenprinting gig posters at night as a way to experiment and get my hands dirty. Eventually, this led me to developing my illustration style and hand lettering."

"I started noticing these great art prints pasted all over town of just random stuff," Gough continues. "It was all coming out of Space 1026. I began checking out the shows every month, seeing Fort Thunder, Shepard Fairey—all that stuff really opened my eyes to screenprinting. That eventually led to becoming a member of Space, printing there for two years."

Gough has supplied imagery to every sort of publication, from *The New York Times* to *Bust*, from *PC Magazine* to *Swindle*. He also publishes the limited-edition zine *Cut and Paste*, which features a collection of personal drawings and doodles.

ROCKY GRIMES

The art of Rocky Grimes is a direct challenge to the easily digested, the mass produced and the shallow. His style is direct and confrontational, in the manner of a Xeroxed flier circa '78.

His do-it-yourself methodology is one that is becoming rare in this day of the quick buck, mass efficiency and max profit, and he believes this process is key. "I feel that the method in which I print and the method in which I create images and hand-build and burn my screens is important to the outcome of my work," he says. "It is an assurance that the end outcome of my work is a closer representation and a purer extension of me. If I screw up a screen, I can accept the results as my own versus paying for my screens to be built by someone else that will always deliver me a perfect, un-warped, blemish-free silkscreen to use, consequently erasing a portion of me from the process of my own work."

Grimes was born in South Carolina and moved to the Florida Keys as a youngster. He and his friends would take trips to Miami to check out what counter-culture and punk rock they could find, and he is still influenced by those experiences today. "The lessons, energy and visual references that I built growing up in the punk and hardcore community seep through to aid in the outcome of my work," he says.

For 2008's Art Basel, Grimes took to the streets and performed live screenprinting as part of an interactive installation called RAW. "Printing live is just an extension of what I do privately, but in a public setting," he says. "The goal is to be honest about my process and to take part as an active participant in a performance, sharing the experience with an individual or group of individuals. Certainly, with anything done live, there is an energy and style delivered to the audience. This is another form of expression that arises out of human interaction in a live environment while creating spontaneous compositions with separate layered screenprinted images, where I treat the silkscreen more as an extension of my body than as a fixed object capable of only being used in a sterile and formulaic way."

GUNSHO

Gunsho, the moniker of James Quigley, sleep-walks and finds himself "standing up in my bed-room in the middle of the night hallucinating on a weekly basis. I don't record them all, but some of them stand out in my memories so much that I end up sketching out some of the elements and usually incorporate them into my work." These nighttime hallucinations and the "Ars Goetia," the first part of the demonology book *The Lesser Key of Solomon*, play a major role in his work. In 2006, Quigley started working on "Gunsho's Demonology," a massive project that reinterprets the 72 demons in the book into contemporary forms. "I'm choosing to present the demons as washed-up, greasy mutations because a believable interpretation can only come about by presenting them as a group of beings among many that have been lurking in our mythological wasteland," he says. Each demon is then turned into a screenprint.

Along with the demons from the "Goetia," Quigley's work often features monsters, beasts or mutants drawn in a style influenced by pop culture of the '70s and '80s. "I'm happy to consider my work lowbrow and be part of a collective interpretation of the culture that raised me and other people in my generation—

MAD magazine, Marvel Comics, TV cartoons and metal and punk record covers were my most accessible artistic products, and those mediums were where I escaped to while growing up in a relatively rural area," he says. "I don't get off on most art, but I still get off on crazy comic-book-art horror movies." Quigley admits he watches a few movies a day. "I always have a movie on when I'm drawing," he says. "Making films is something I've been pouring a lot of energy into, and I've been teaching myself mask-making and monster makeup."

A few years ago, Quigley decided to dedicate himself to his art full time. "I never had an artistic agenda until I got to know other people who are very similar and who put creativity at the forefront of their lives regardless of whether it was financially fruitful," he explains. "I think I just figured that I had a choice to just manage to get by money-wise working jobs that I hated, or I could try being just as broke being an artist but doing what I enjoy. It was a pretty simple decision."

Quigley has worked with *Tokion*, *Complex*, Heroin Skateboards, éS Footwear and a number of record labels and bands.

STEVEN HARRINGTON

In Steven Harrington's work, mismatched illustrations of spider webs, ampersands and fruit combine to form colorful patterns that playfully address social ties. The objects, drawn inside triangles and squares, occasionally spill over and are laid out in a way that recalls a puzzle or the children's game "Chutes and Ladders."

Native American symbols such as feathers and tee-pees also play a major role. "I feel these symbols and icons very much represent a strong sense of social community and connectivity," Harrington says. "I guess incorporating these symbols into my work is just my way of trying to reflect a sense of community and connection amongst my viewers. A little of it has to do with past times, and maybe it also has something to do with growing up with a hippie mom and a pair of hippie aunts."

Harrington grew up in La Verne, California, a suburb just east of Los Angeles. His high school art teacher encouraged him to pursue art, and he went on to attend the Art Center College of Design in Pasadena.

Harrington's work has been shown around the world; his traveling art show "Our Mountain" made stops in France, Germany, Italy and Spain. A full-color companion book of work from the show was also released.

In addition, he and Justin Krietemeyer run the full-service design agency National Forest. Harrington's work has graced skate decks for Element Skateboards, been turned into a toy as part of a collaboration with Kid Robot, and printed on mugs and dinner plates for Urban Outfitters. "Lately I've been really into the idea of reproducing the same image in multiple mediums," he says. "If it looks nice on a T-shirt and people embrace it, then why can't it be a poster too? Most of my work happens to be designed for screen-printing, so I have no problem printing it over and over and over."

Somehow, we all seem connected.

CODY HUDSON

Cody Hudson hails from Wisconsin, where he started making art at an early age, embellishing his board's grip tape and making skate zines. Rather than attend a pricey art school, Hudson opted for a two-year technical college, where he learned how to do wax paste-up layouts and draw type by hand. After graduating, he got a job filling in animation cells of Sparky the Fire Dog, and, later, laying out ads at a weekly coupon magazine. He then moved around the country—Vermont, Miami, New Jersey—gaining experience from a variety of design jobs, until he settled down in Chicago.

Now he runs his own design company, Struggle Inc., through which he has designed countless album covers, T-shirts and books. Hudson balances commercial work with personal art, paintings and large-scale installations.

In his screenprints and paintings, Hudson relies on the graphic, using playful shapes and basic iconography such as half circles and protest fists. In a print for Upper Playground's Obama series, Hudson's simple, anaglyphic letters send a bold message.

Hudson is also known for his indoor and outdoor installations, which are often made out of wood harvested from neighborhood dumpsters. In 2006, Hudson was commissioned by the City of Chicago Public Art Program to create a permanent installation at the Sox-35th CTA station as part of the Arts in Transit Program.

In 2007, he exhibited at the Museum of Contemporary Art in Chicago. Fifty24SF recently released *Save My Life*, a book that compiles his designs, drawings and photos from the past two years.

Libérez

l'Humanité

contemporary leisure

spaceship earth, i think i love you.

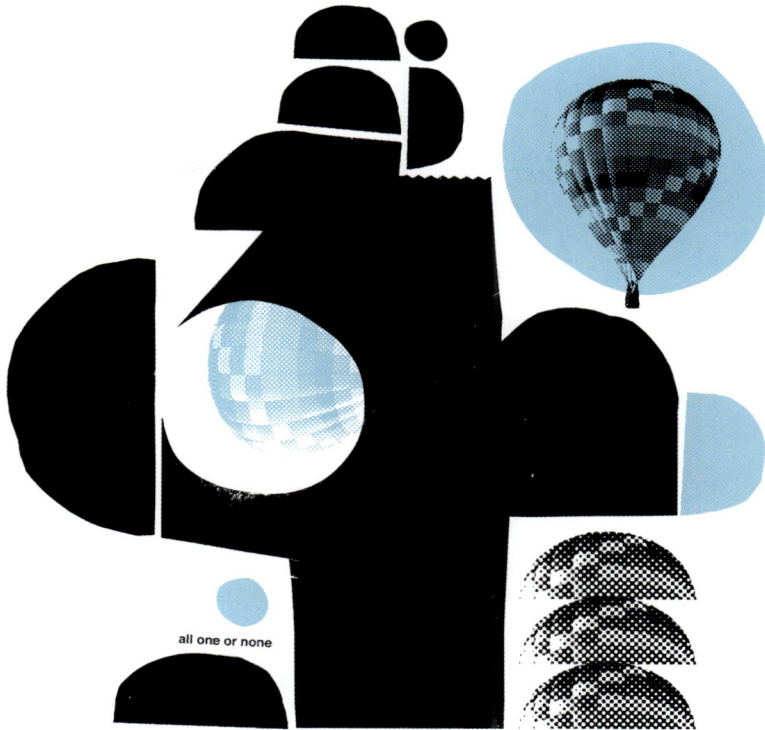

all one or none

country girl, i think you're pretty

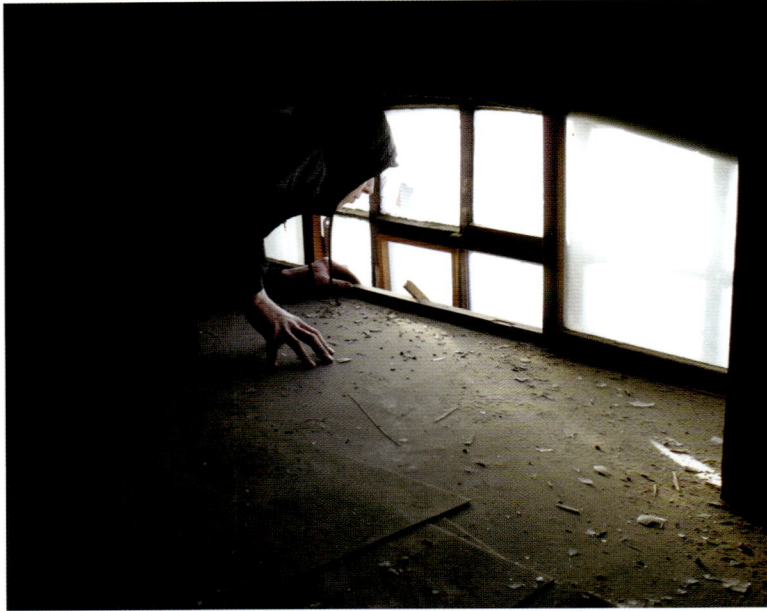

PAUL INSECT

Paul Insect is a London-based artist whose cutting viewpoint on modern life has resulted in a controversial body of work. Insect uses screenprinting, Xerox, collage, spray paint, acrylic, sculpture and the streets of the urban core to get his messages across. Political satire, celebrity skewering, icon destruction, gun violence, consumerism, human rights, greed, war and the hubris of the superpowers all come under the scrutiny of Insect.

A vein of humor runs through the serious overtones of his work, injecting surprise and vibrancy. For his "Bullion" project, Insect worked with a metal foundry to create faux gold bullion. "It was like being back in the Dark Ages," Insect told *Juxtapoz* in a 2007 interview. "They didn't have e-mail; I could only write letters or call them on the phone. So I would have to take the train up to Bradford every so often to see how things were going, which was always a strange experience. From the first meeting, when I left them my model of the bar, to when they cast gold ingots for me ... and at the same time, being really sketchy about what I was going to do with them." Insect placed the gold bars on top of waste bins and freeway dividers in London. "Bullion" was also the name of his solo exhibit at Lazarides Gallery, as well as an accompanying book.

Insect's work has been featured in books and magazines, shown worldwide and destroyed by city workers making the streets "safe" for tourism.

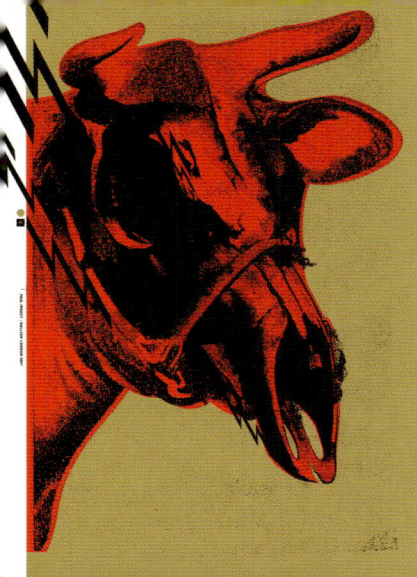

INVISIBLE CREATURE

Don and Ryan Clark, the creative juggernauts behind Invisible Creature, a design studio located in Seattle, Washington, are self-taught brothers who launched the design studio in 2006 after conceiving hundreds of CD packages and silkscreened posters for Asterik Studio. The name Invisible Creature came from the realization that those responsible for the visual identities of so many recognizable names were hidden from the public.

The work produced by Invisible Creature is the result of their easy partnership. "We work together on everything," Don told *Grain Edit* in an interview. "We sit three feet from each other and are constantly going over ideas for each project. How can this be better? What would you do differently? What do you think of these color choices? Does this just plain suck? And on and on. I feel like we are always pushing each other to create the best work we possibly can."

As children, the brothers used to "draw and draw and draw some more," and were inspired by their grandfather, an illustrator for NASA. "Life is too short to work a 9-to-5 job that you abhor, and my grandfather was always a gleaming example of someone who got paid to do what they love," Don says. "There was no other option for us—we were going to make the most of this life and if it was art that we loved, it was art that we were going to do."

Their talents not restricted to the visual, the brothers are also part of the metalcore band Demon Hunter. As designer-musicians, they are able to attend to their clients' needs from an insider's point of view; in 2008, they received their fourth Grammy nomination for design work on the *Hawk Nelson Is My Friend* album.

Recently, they stepped away from for-hire work with a gallery show titled "Haven." "The experience was an exciting one," Don says. "We strive for quality and integrity each time we start a new project. We want to just continue pushing ourselves in every aspect of art and design. We pour so much of ourselves into every little thing we do, and I never want that to end."

BRIGHT EYES

PLUS JIM JAMES
(OF MY MORNING JACKET)
AND M. WARD

TUESDAY, OCTOBER 19TH / THE COMMODORE BALLROOM
$22 / 8:00 PM / ALL AGES

POISON THE WELL + EVERY TIME I DIE + THE BRONX
NORA + CODESEVEN WINTER 2003

BRAND NEW
FALL TOUR 2003

MONDAY, APRIL 24 SEATTLE CHOP SUEY + TUESDAY, APRIL 25 PORTLAND BERBATI'S PAN $14
HARD-FI & THE RAKES

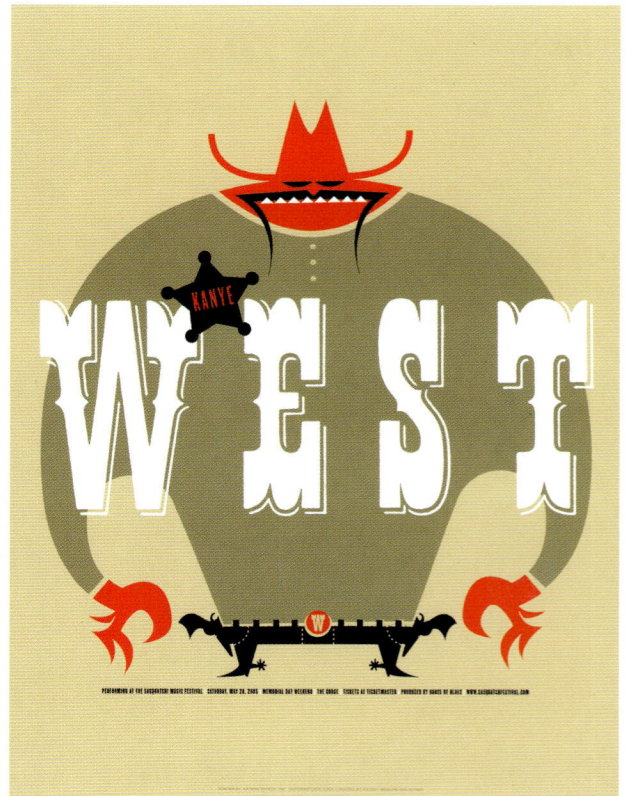

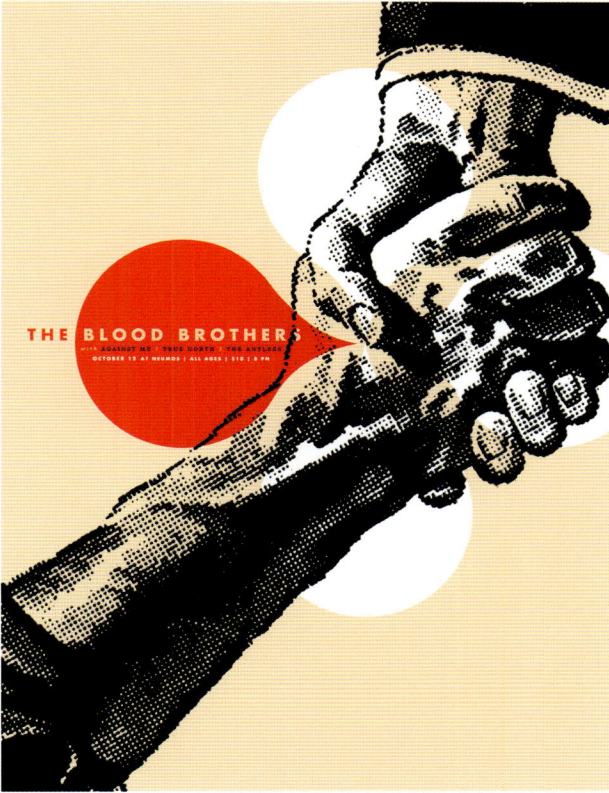

spiritualized®

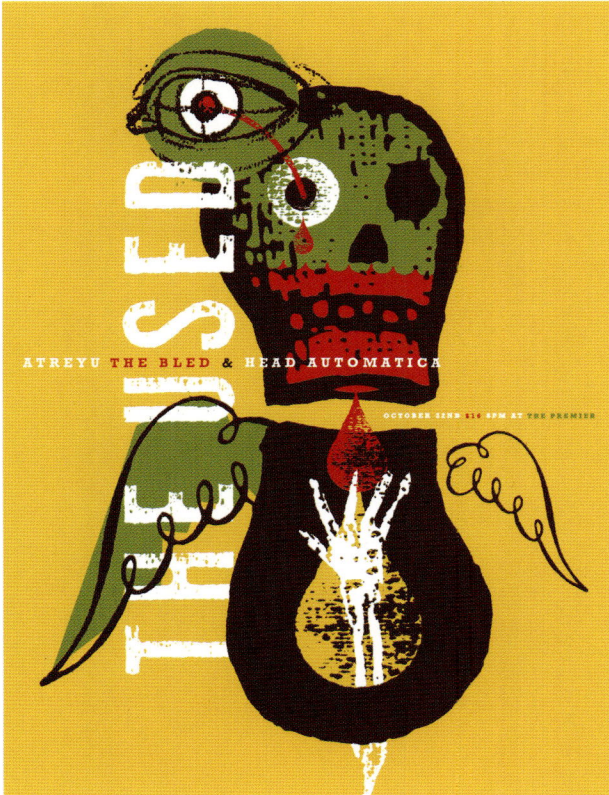

ATREYU THE BLED & HEAD AUTOMATICA

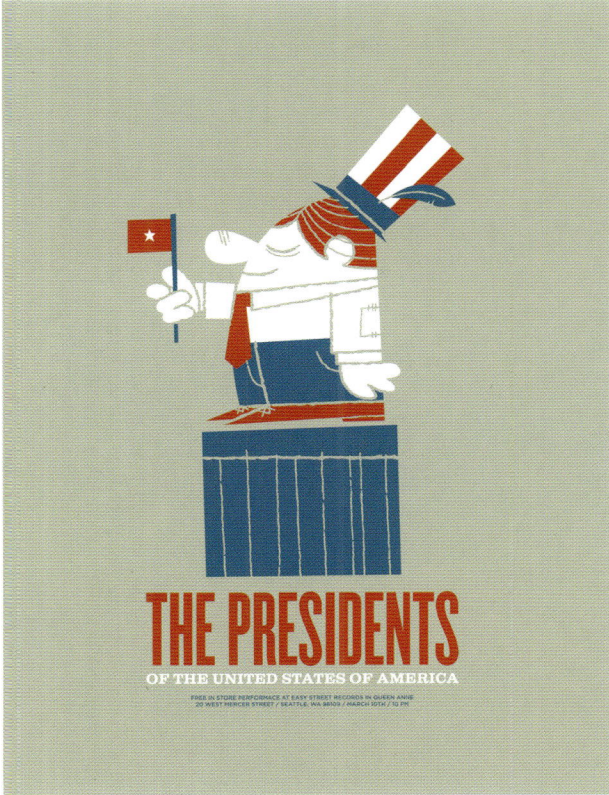

THE PRESIDENTS
OF THE UNITED STATES OF AMERICA

JEFF KLEINSMITH

Jeff Kleinsmith began freelancing for Sub Pop Records in 1992, and within two years he became the label's art director, a job he has maintained ever since, continuously sharpening his design skills by working on hundreds of poster and packaging projects. Kleinsmith and Jesse LeDoux co-own Patent Pending Industries, a design and screenprinting shop Kleinsmith founded in '92. His work brings to mind movie posters of the 1960s, pulp novels of the '50s and the classic design of Blue Note Records. He is known for his use of open space, appropriate type treatments, tasteful color combinations and found objects.

He cites motivation as having "been inspired by so many things over the years, including punk rock album covers and fliers, to high-end design by the masters such as Paul Rand, Art Chantry, Saul Bass, Push Pin Studios, etc. The thread that runs through all of my inspirations is that I'm mostly interested in design from the past as opposed to what's going on currently."

Regarding methodology, he observes, "It's pretty common for low tech to emerge as a backlash against times of high tech. To use music analogies: Punk rock erupted as a backlash against disco; grunge exploded as a backlash against high-gloss hair bands. I think it's a similar thing here where screenprinting and letterpress have a low-tech appeal in a world dominated by high tech, high speed, text messaging—all great stuff, but it shows that as humans we still want to touch stuff and look at it up close."

Kleinsmith lives in Seattle, Washington, with his wife, two daughters and dogs.

WILCO

NEW YORK CITY IRVING PLAZA W / SPECIAL GUESTS JUNE 8, 2004

DESIGN BY JEFF KLEINSMITH (PATENT PENDING). PRINTED BY PATENT PENDING PRESS.

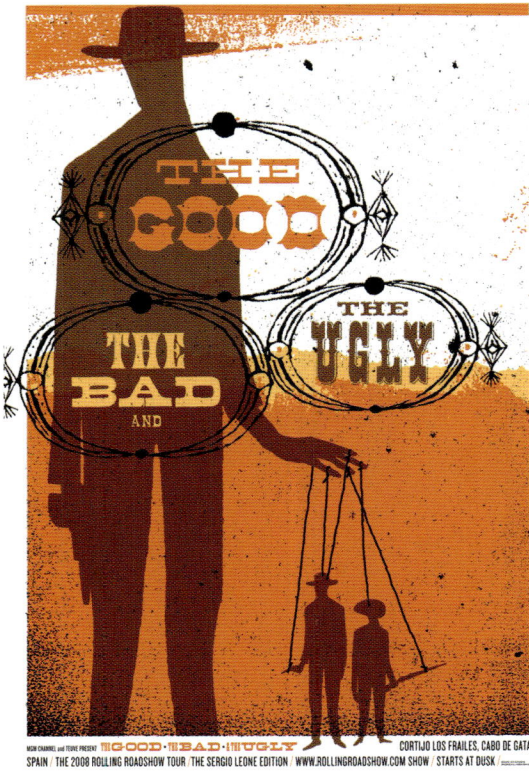

The Good, The Bad and The Ugly

MGM CHANNEL and TERVE PRESENT THE GOOD THE BAD & THE UGLY / CORTIJO LOS FRAILES, CABO DE GATA
SPAIN / THE 2008 ROLLING ROADSHOW TOUR / THE SERGIO LEONE EDITION / WWW.ROLLINGROADSHOW.COM SHOW / STARTS AT DUSK

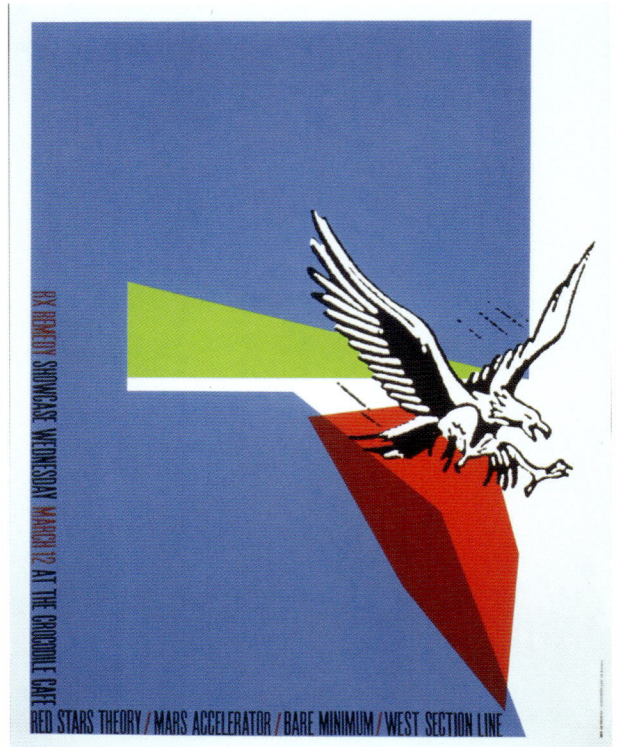

RX REMEDY SHOWCASE WEDNESDAY MARCH 12 AT THE CROCODILE CAFE
RED STARS THEORY / MARS ACCELERATOR / BARE MINIMUM / WEST SECTION LINE

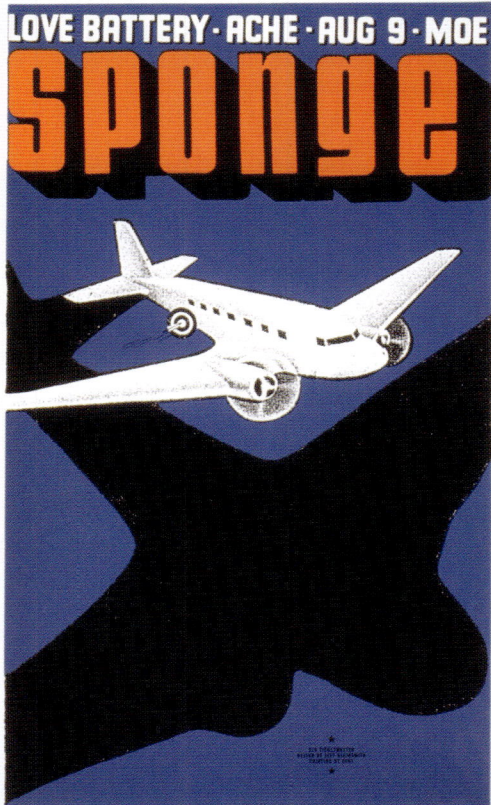

LOVE BATTERY · ACHE · AUG 9 · MOE
Sponge

WIDE SPREAD PANIC
WOODLANDS
WOODLANDS, TEXAS FRIDAY MARCH 23RD 2007

Feb. 6 - March 29 / The Art Gallery at the University of Maryland / Opening reception (Feb. 6th 5-7pm)
Sweet Booth (sales event on Feb. 6 from 11am - 7:30pm)
John Foster's gallery lecture on March 5 at 3pm (called Sweet: John Foster Talks about the Art of the Contemporary Rock Poster)

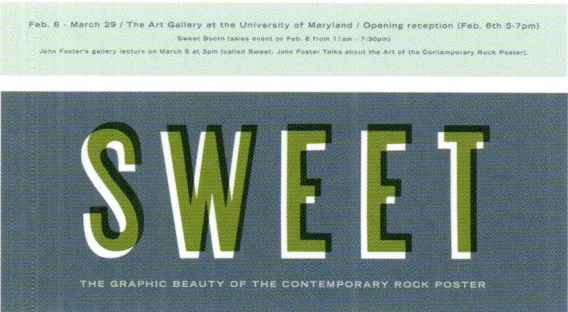

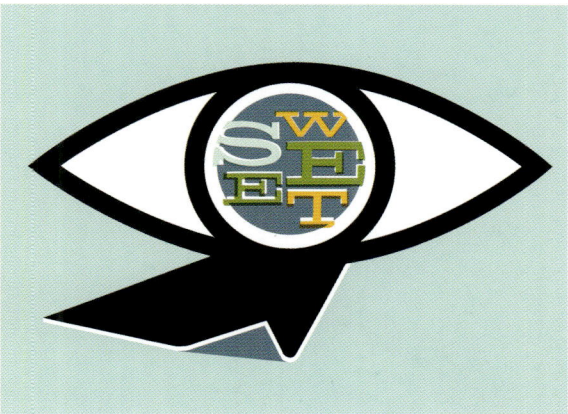

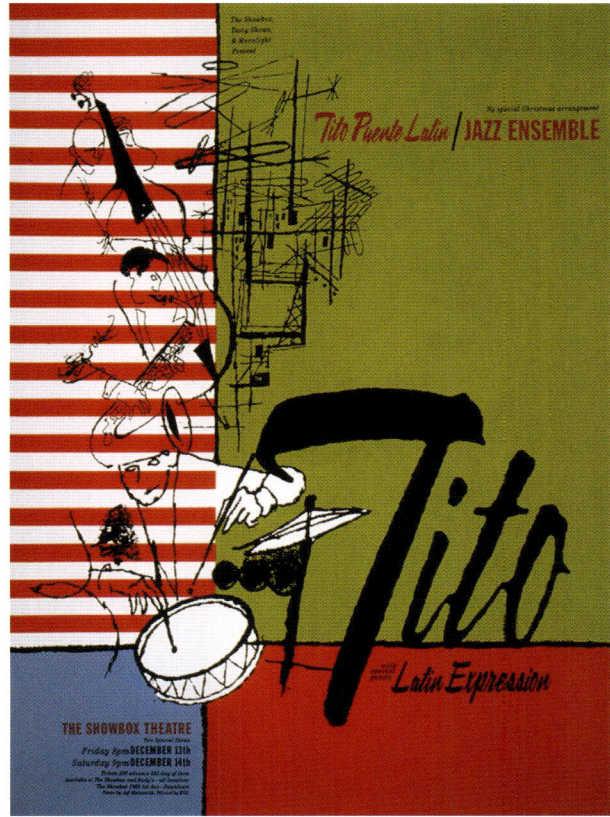

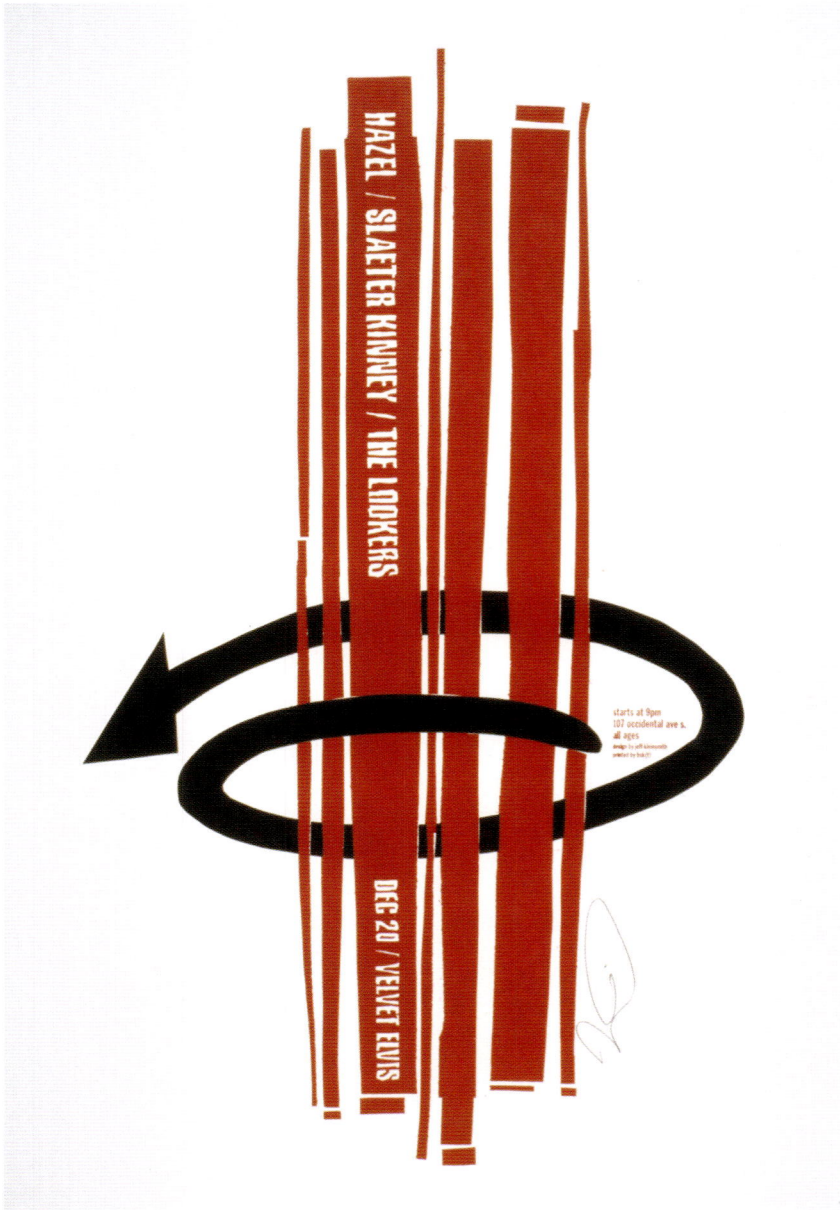

HAZEL / SLAETER KINNEY / THE LOOKERS

starts at 9pm
107 occidental ave s.
all ages

DEC 20 / VELVET ELVIS

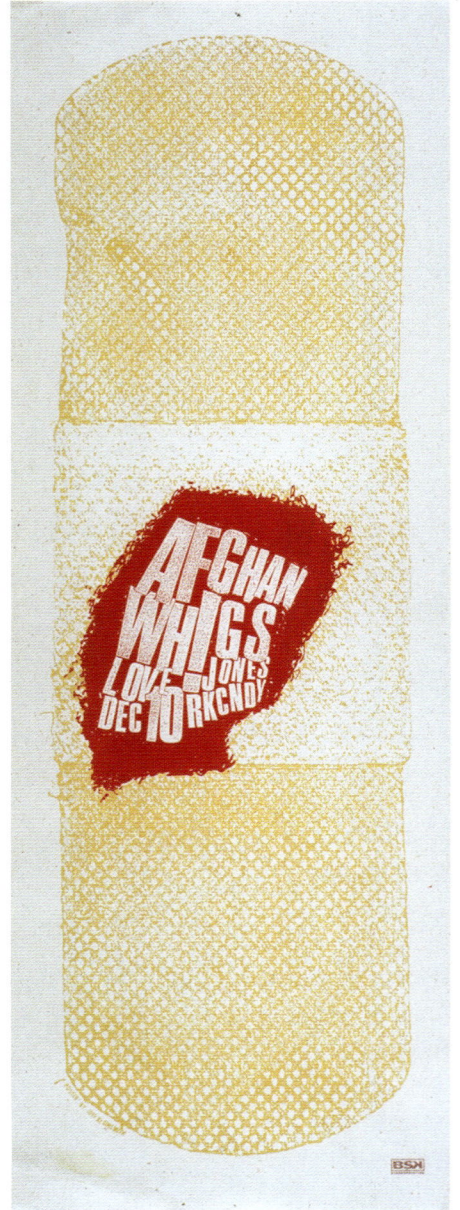

AFGHAN WHIGS
LOVE JONES
DEC 10 RKCNDY

JUSTIN KRIETEMEYER

Justin Krietemeyer always wanted to be an artist. "I don't think I ever really thought of being anything else," he said in an interview on the website *Neu Black*. "My mom was an artist, and I'd always grown up around art. So when it came time to decide what I wanted to go to school for, it was obvious that it was the thing I was best at."

Krietemeyer attended Art Center College of Design in Pasadena, California, and after graduating, started a design shop, National Forest, with friend and collaborator Steven Harrington. "A lot of people graduate school and go get a job, and ask me, 'How do you do it and not have money?'" Krietemeyer told *Neu Black*. "But the reality was we were already broke. We didn't get jobs, make a bunch of money, buy a nice car, and then think about quitting that job to start our own thing. We just started where we were."

Today, National Forest is a full-service design agency. Krietemeyer and Harrington have worked on countless projects—from designing the Urban Outfit-ters catalog to creating a mural and installation at the Standard hotel in downtown Los Angeles. "We have a constant conversation running about where we are going now and what are we doing next," Krietemeyer told *Neu Black*. "It keeps us excited because National Forest keeps growing into something bigger than just Steve and Justin individually."

In his personal work, Krietemeyer displays an affinity for the retro. One series of paintings is on van conversions, and another is on his favorite mixtapes (cassettes labeled Stevie Wonder, Michael Jackson, the Doors and NWA are just a few). In one of his transfers on found paper stock, a giant moon looms above a lively crowd, evoking the primal, Dionysian freedom of the '60s.

When *Neu Black* asked whom he admired, Krietemeyer answered, "anybody who's able to make art and love what they're doing without compromising their soul."

LARGEMAMMAL

The creative outlet of Kevin Mercer, Largemammal is able to cover a vast editorial and design space, producing a staggering array of imagery. Brushwork, typography, hand-drawn type, calligraphy, collage, original drawings, pencil and pen all conflagrate with sharp composition. Mercer claims a variety of influences: Cy Twombly's "50 Days at Iliam," R. Buckminster Fuller's vitality and Edouard Vuillard's sense of color. Of Robert Rauschenberg, he asks, "How can any screenprinter not be inspired by him?"

No matter what the design challenges are, Mercer squarely hits the mark when it comes to matching a band's sound with color, imagery and composition. "Leading up to the design, I'll listen to a band carefully to see if there is some kind of visual marker that I can draw from it," he says. "I see a difference between just listening to a record and actually hearing it. There is much more emotional, spiritual and mental content in great music than I can express on paper, so I try to find one aspect to focus on for each piece. When they serve their purpose, I'm hoping that they offer the concertgoer, listener or collector a way to attach that image to whatever experience they had in seeing, hearing or collecting the band's music."

Mercer remembers the creative urge surfacing when he was just a kid: "My first artistic memory is sitting on my grandfather's lap with a little chalkboard, drawing pictures of trucks with him. I somewhat always knew that I wanted to do something creative. There wasn't even a decision to make. So when I went to college I had to decide a slightly more specific path in fine art. Painting and printmaking really decided that path at first. Then the need for gainful employment decided the path into graphic work." Mercer's work has been shown in solo and group exhibitions, printed in books like *The Art of Modern Rock* and *SWAG 2*, and represented artists as diverse as the Melvins and Daniel Johnston.

JANUARY 31 THEATER OF LIVING ARTS PHILADELPHIA

THE ARCADE FIRE

WITH FINAL FANTASY and MAN MAN

WALKMEN
ROCKWELL
MAZARIN

FRIDAY, MAY 26 AT 9PM
THE THEATER OF THE LIVING ARTS
PRESENTED BY ELECTRIC FACTORY CONCERTS

JESSE LeDOUX

Jesse LeDoux worked for years at Sub Pop Records, producing packaging for releases on the label; his efforts on the Shins' *Chutes Too Narrow* even earned him a Grammy nomination. "Working at Sub Pop provided me with an experimental foundation in which to grow," he says. "They were small enough that I could talk the marketing department into my many bad/rad ideas (pop-up hand-assembled LP jacket for Damien Jurado? Awesome!), and they were large enough that what I made would be seen by a lot of people." Today, he splits his time between Providence, Rhode Island, and Tokyo, creating and designing under his LeDouxville imprint.

LeDoux also travels the country, engaged in teaching and creating gallery installations, such as the "Masters of Balance" installation he did at the University of Maryland. "I love working at a large scale," he says. "The environments I create are much more convincing when experienced in life-sized proportions." In conjunction with Kidrobot, LeDoux released an innovative line of toys called the "Critter Splitters," which can be taken apart and recombined in any number of ways to create new characters.

Observing that his art is about "escaping everyday life and climbing into a new one," LeDoux continues, "I think my work is my way of dealing with the lame parts of reality by creating an alternate world. Unfortunate events still happen in the environments I create. The difference is how they are dealt with. In real life, the dude who steals your laptop will probably sell it for a fraction of what it's worth, and will most likely get away. In my world, he'll be caught. His hands will be cut off and replaced with clouds. Then, he will be forced to punch himself in the face for all eternity. It makes more sense to me."

THE LITTLE FRIENDS OF PRINTMAKING

The Little Friends of Printmaking embrace an aesthetic that combines the curvaceous figures and tongue-in-cheek humor of R. Crumb with '70s balloon writing and imagery reminiscent of the children's television classic *Schoolhouse Rock*. The Little Friends are JW and Melissa Buchanan, a married couple from Milwaukee, Wisconsin, who have embraced a rock-and-roll attitude toward screenprinting, holding exhibitions and artists' residencies all over the country and once even packing into a van to exhibit their art on tour.

"When we were just starting out, we traveled cross-country with Seripop, putting on exhibitions and art events," JW says. "I think we did 25 dates over five weeks. That set the tone for Melissa and I. We realized that we could go do an exhibition anywhere. Now we can be fearless."

Melissa continues, "It started out as a thing where we had said, 'The bands get to go on tour, why not us?' We'd get into town and set up a show. Sometimes the gallery people would have it set up beforehand, but usually it was up to us. Then, the opening would be that night, and sometimes the opening was the closing too. We'd take down the show and sleep on the gallery floor. There probably wouldn't be a Little Friends without that tour."

The pair collaborates on every project. "There are many components to what we do, but the most crucial ones are coming up with the concept sketches, and the printing process," JW says. "Those are two things we always do together. Nothing ever gets started or finished without both of our approval."

Melissa adds, "It's important for us to work closely together, because we want all of our work to speak for both of us as a team."

The Little Friends of Printmaking have been featured in *New Masters of Poster Design* and *Handmade Nation*. They were named "Young Guns" by the Art Director's Club and have won awards for excellence in advertising from *Communication Arts*. JW and Melissa have been working together since 1999, been married since 2000, and show no signs of stopping.

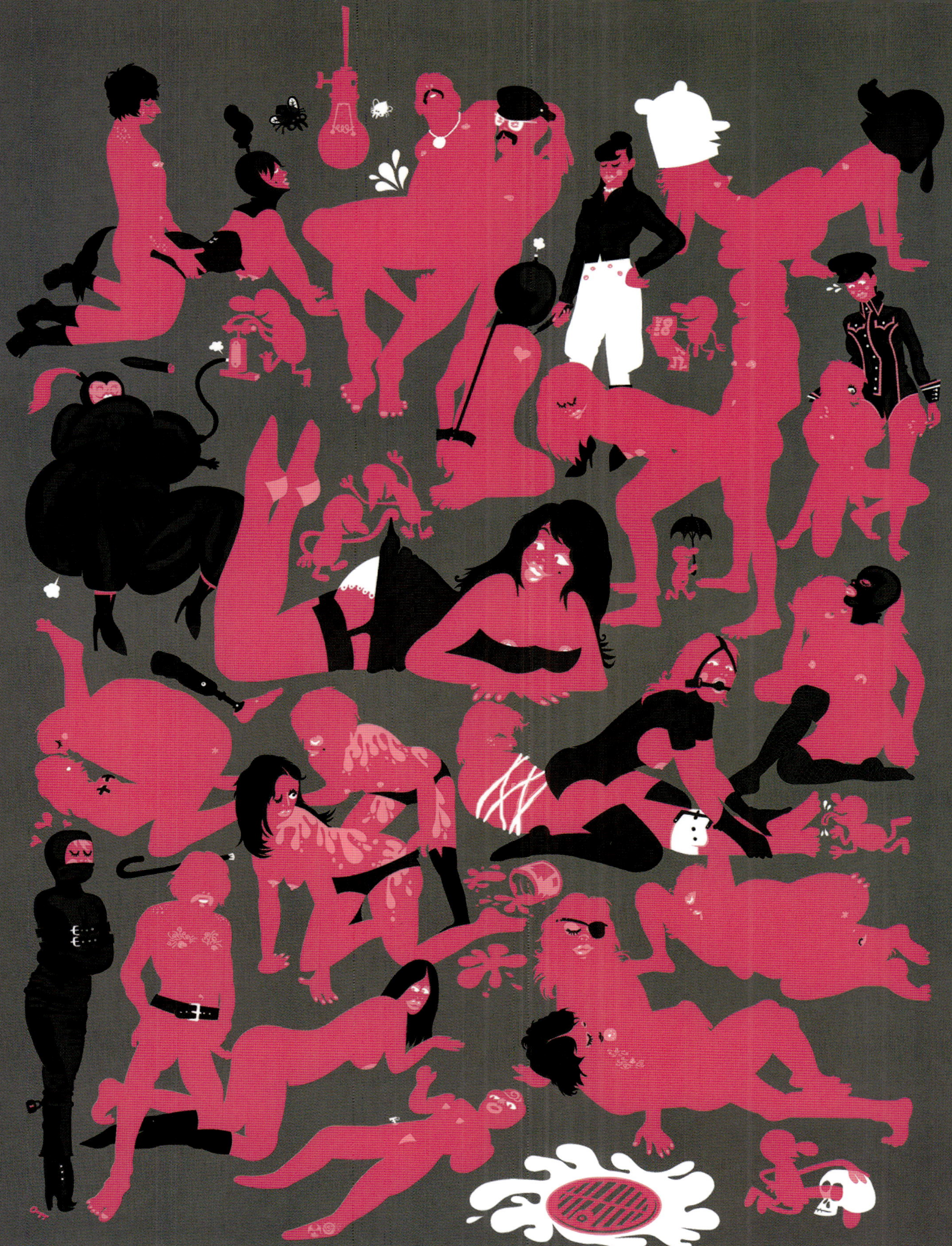

Core77 presents:
Design, Wit, and the Creative Act
Friday, November 9th, 2007
YOUR MODERATOR ZE FRANK
A PANEL DISCUSSION AT THE
Art Directors Club
106 W. 29th Street New York, NY
DOORS OPEN 1:00PM
2:00 PRESENTATIONS
COCKTAILS 5:00
AUTHOR STEVEN HELLER
TECHNOLOGIST KELLY DOBSON
ARTIST TOBIAS WONG
KIDROBOT PAUL BUDNITZ
VISIT core77.com/offsite

NOISE POP
2008
S.F., CALIF.

NADA SURF
THE JEALOUS GIRLFRIENDS
Friday, April 4, 2008
8:30PM
Metro • 3730 North Clark St • Chicago, IL

the Comedians of Comedy
AWESOME
laffs
PATTON OSWALT
MARIA BAMFORD
BRIAN POSEHN
AND LOTS OF SPECIAL GUESTS
2007 TOUR
HA HA
POSTER BY THE LITTLE FRIENDS OF PRINTMAKING
the COMEDIANS of COMEDY TOUR 2007
OCT 03 SEATTLE, WA
OCT 05 PORTLAND, OR
OCT 06 LOS ANGELES, CA
OCT 10 SAN DIEGO, CA
OCT 11 LAS VEGAS, NV
OCT 25 BOSTON, MA
OCT 26 READING, PA
OCT 27 NEW YORK, NY
OCT 28 PHILADELPHIA, PA
OCT 30 PITTSBURGH, PA
NOV 01 CHICAGO, IL
NOV 02 ANN ARBOR, MI
NOV 03 BUFFALO, NY
NOV 04 CLEVELAND, OH
NOV 05 LOUISVILLE, KY
NOV 06 BLOOMINGTON, IN
NOV 08 MINNEAPOLIS, MN
NOV 30 SAN FRANCISCO, CA

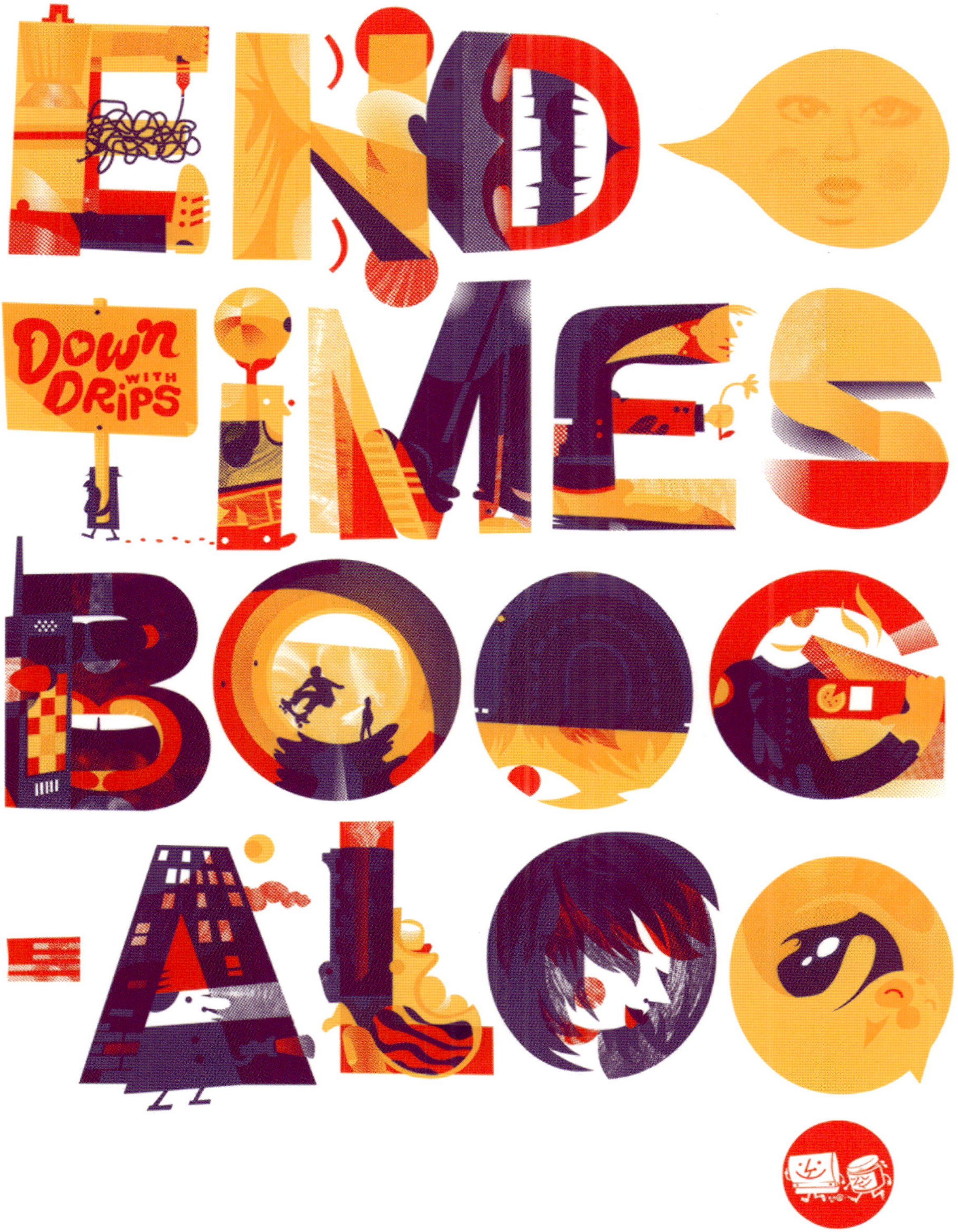
Down
WITH
DRIPS

THE BIRD'S THE WORD

Pink Flamingos

AN EXERCISE IN BAD TASTE

DESPERATE LIVING

IT'S NOT PRETTY

Polyester

PRESENTED IN GLORIOUS *Odorama*

BLACK BOYS

Hefty RIDEAWAY Girl

OOH

UNGH

Hair-Spray

"KIDDEE KLASSIC"

2007 ROLLING ROADSHOW TOUR PRESENTS A
JOHN WATERS DUSK-TIL-DAWN MOVIE MARATHON
Sponsored by **NEW LINE CINEMA** • **DEWAR'S WHITE LABEL** • **AIN'T IT COOL NEWS**
FRIDAY, AUGUST 20TH IN WYMAN PARK TUDOR ARMS AVENUE & 37TH STREET
MOVIES START AT SUNDOWN **BALTIMORE, MARYLAND**
more details at www.rollingroadshow.com

BLAKE E. MARQUIS

Blake Marquis has a clean graphic style that reveals a more complex side when examined closely. Take, for example, the portraits he did for the MySpace.com Secret Stand-up, an ongoing comedy series. These seemingly straightforward portraits are composed of intricate lines that mimic the young tendrils of a flowering vine. Realism is trumped by Marquis' personal style.

Marquis' work often features original typography. "I've always been attracted to type and how it sets the tone in a piece of work," he says. "The playfulness in my type lately is just a phase. I've been really into drawing the letterforms roughly, without using much for guidelines. For a long time I was making these tedious alphabets or logos." Marquis is also known for his elaborate patterns, as exemplified by "Vine Pattern," a sequence of leaves and loops that was painted on a public wall in Los Angeles as part of a project with Shepard Fairey.

His work has enlivened the pages of *The New York Times Magazine*, *ReadyMade* and *Swindle*. The recipient of both a Clio and an Andy Award for his illustration in the *One Show* book, his patterns can also be seen in *Over & Over*, a book about pattern design. Although he is New York based, his illustrations and designs have been exhibited in galleries all over the world, most recently at Subliminal Projects.

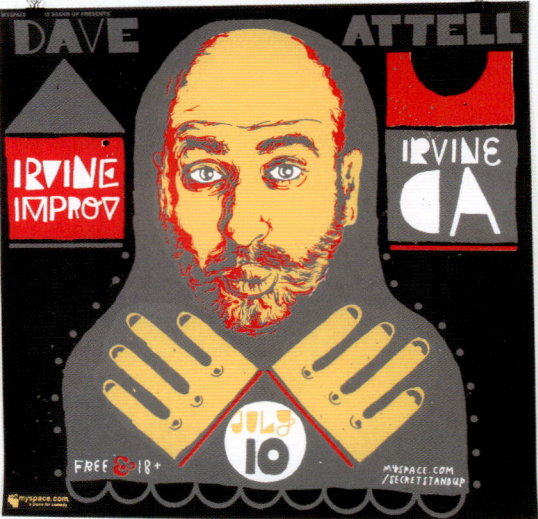

BILL McRIGHT

The intricately lined creatures in Bill McRight's prints are the result of a laborious process. McRight uses shoe polish to draw a silhouette on linoleum, and a chisel to create details. Next he rolls the block with ink, hand-prints the design onto vellum and exposes a screen. Then he begins the normal screenprinting steps.

Although he calls his process "somewhat ridiculous," McRight relishes the craftsmanship of the woodblock technique. "I love the process of carving and figuring out how to create the images," he says. "Every time I carve a block I am thinking about how I can make better cuts, make the images come to life, make it more fun to look at and solve new problems. I guess part of what makes me choose this process is the challenge and fun of creating problems for myself and then discovering how I can fix them."

His hand-carved lines add texture and depth to his prints, which have an almost ancient feel. "I also really like the fact that I am sitting down and using my hands to directly create an image," he says. "Cutting a block becomes almost a kind of ritual that involves me sitting down, clearing my head and digging into the block. I feel connected to a tradition that was around far before I was—and will hopefully be around long after I'm gone."

McRight was raised on the southern tier of the Eastern Seaboard. He first tried printmaking while earning his BFA at Winthrop University in South Carolina, but didn't take it seriously until he saw what friend Dennis McNett was doing with linoleum. McRight went on to earn his MFA in printmaking at Pratt Institute in New York.

Now a denizen of Philadelphia, McRight is a member of the renowned Space 1026 collective. His work has been published in magazines such as *Everyone is Awesome All the Time*, *Time Out New York* and *Real Raw*. His art has graced the walls of galleries and adorns the bottom of decks made by Saturday Skateboards. He currently teaches printmaking at liberal arts school Arcadia University.

If all the ink in the world suddenly dried up, McRight says he would "figure out papermaking and crush up some berries and shit and guard that stuff."

SATURDAY

SATURDAY

SATURDAY

SATURDAY

SATURDAY

SATURDAY

SATURDAY

Saturday

Saturday

SATURDAY

Saturday

SATURDAY

SATURDAY

SATURDAY

SATURDAY

SATURDAY

SATURDAY

Saturday

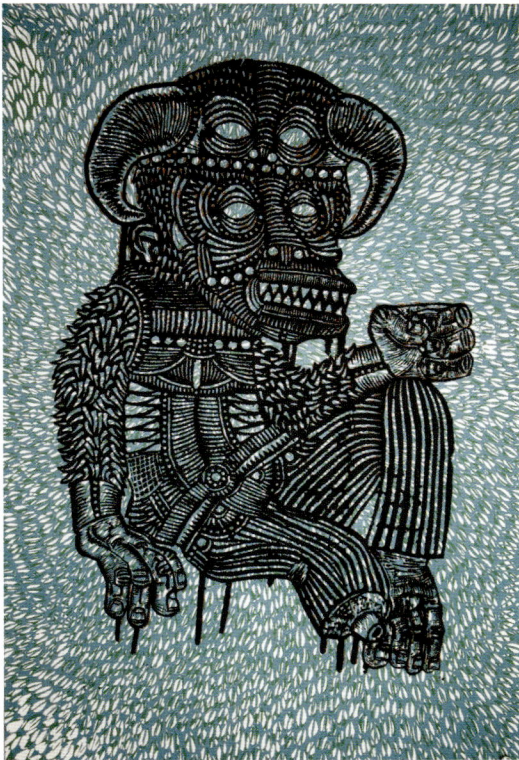
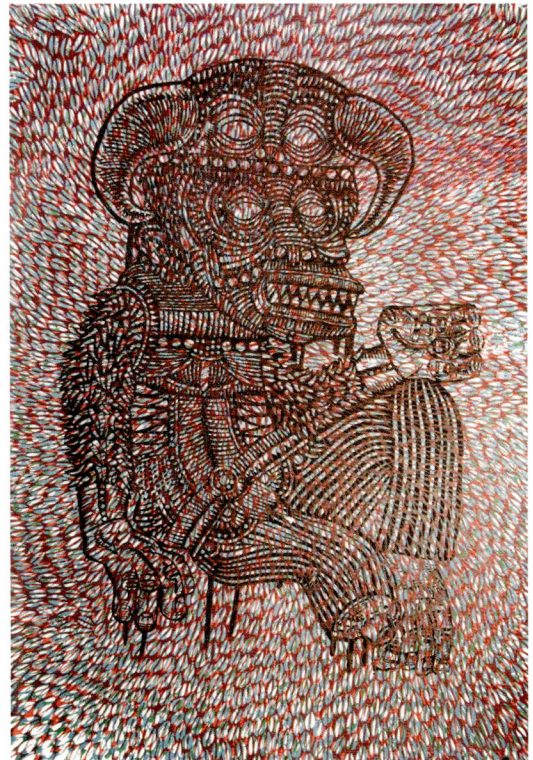

MICHAEL MOTORCYCLE

Michael Motorcycle draws in the style of a Victorian children's book in overdrive. His work combines elements from the turn of the 20th century—namely art nouveau and Alphonse Mucha's flowing designs—with 1960s psychedelic posters. "I think first and foremost my work is romantic," Motorcycle says. "A little melancholy too. In regard to style, mine is always changing. I tweak things just a little bit with every poster in order to keep things interesting."

In describing the meaning of his work, he muses, "I'm not always sure what the symbolism means until some time has passed—sometimes not even then. A lot of it revolves around love. A couple of years ago, I lost a good friend. There was a lot of blood then. In one of my favorites, there is a Victorian steam man floating in a boat on an ocean of blood. In the bloody water there are two men with stars for heads. In the Sonic Youth poster that followed, the star men are magnified so that you can see what they are holding and what they are saying. Most people don't realize that they are connected until I point it out. Watching that moment of discovery is a lot of fun for me."

The process "all starts out with a line drawing. Up until very recently I did all my color separations by hand with a brush and film ink on clear acetate. That got to be way too tedious and time consuming, so I purchased a large format ink-jet printer. I do all my color separations in Photoshop now. I don't think I would have been able to do it this way if I hadn't started out doing it all by hand."

"This summer I went to Portugal and did the separations in my hotel room. That is something I never could have done before. I would have been glued to my drawing board for a week or more covered in black ink."

"I generally print seven or eight colors. I can get 14 or 15 different colors from mixing seven or eight colors directly on the paper. I also print split fountains on most of my colors. It takes a lot of skill to keep the colors where I want them on the paper because the ink shifts with each pass."

Born in New Mexico, Motorcycle has lived in Southern California since the age of 9. He now lives in Pasadena with his wife and cats. Along with screenprinting, Motorcycle also paints and plays music. He is about to move into a larger studio, where he hopes to teach screenprinting to others.

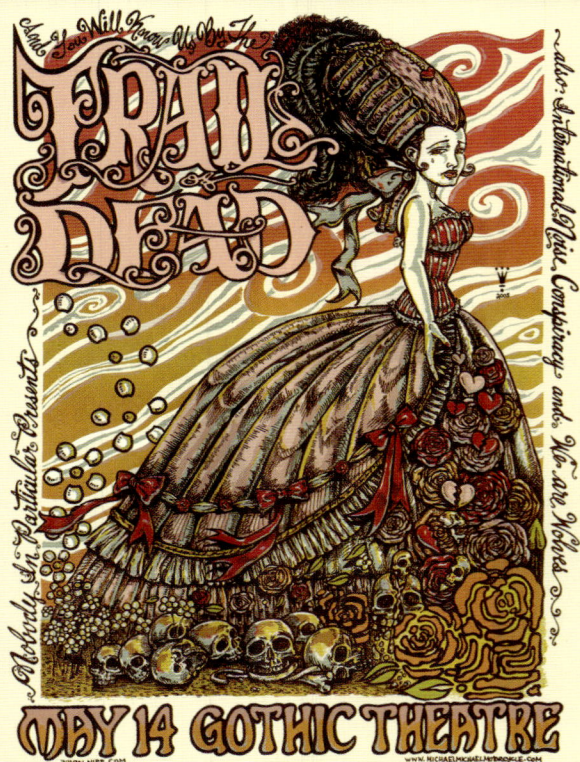

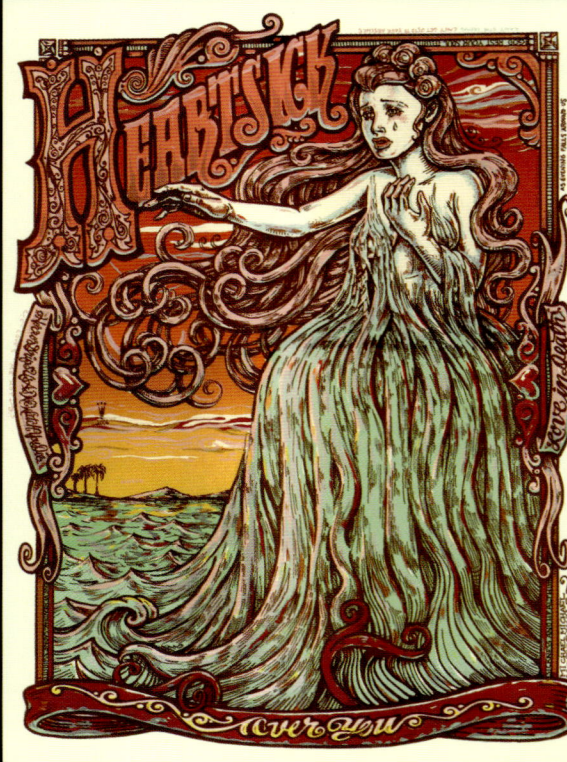

NOBODY · IN · PARTICULAR · PRESENTS

DANZIG

WWW.NIPP.COM

2005

WWW.MICHAELMICHAELMOTORCYCLE.COM

MARCH 11

OGDEN THEATRE

WITH ~ KATAKLYSM ~ EYES OF FIRE ~ 7 PM

JASON MUNN

In 2003, Wisconsin native Jason Munn opened Small Stakes, a design studio in Oakland, California where music posters, packaging, book covers and T-shirts are created for clients all over the world. Munn's work is a careful combination of graphic elements, open space and limited color. "Most of my work—whether an album package, magazine illustration or anything else—could easily be silkscreened, even though it is offset-printed," he says. "I've always been attracted to one-to-three-color design that is simple and idea-based."

He cites skateboarding as a major design influence. "As a kid I was always drawing, and what I responded to the most was skateboard graphics and album covers—this was where I discovered art in design," he says. "I feel skateboard graphics and T-shirts were a huge influence on the way I work now—all the early graphics being silkscreened, and the amount that was done with a few colors has always stuck with me."

Nature—in the form of trees, feathers and flowers—is another hallmark of Munn's work. "For a lot of the quieter bands I've done work for, I often use natural elements as a starting point," he says. "Single natural elements seemed to work well with sparse music, and I've always liked the combination." Munn also plays with shape and form, employing multistable figures: In a poster for Noise Pop's 15th anniversary, the wings of a bird are composed of high-rise buildings. In other works, a comb morphs into a gun, and the state of Idaho transforms into a grand piano.

Munn's art is a part of the permanent collection at the San Francisco Museum of Modern Art and has been featured in magazines such as *Print*, *Communication Arts* and *ReadyMade*.

TED LEO + PHARMACISTS

GEORGIE JAMES | SO MANY DYNAMOS | PONY COME LATELY

MARCH 2, 2007 | GREAT AMERICAN MUSIC HALL | NOISE POP 15

THE SHINS
27 MARCH 2007 at MANCHESTER ACADEMY

THE BOOKS
GREAT AMERICAN MUSIC HALL
APRIL 17, 2006
W/ CLOGR

LOW
SEPTEMBER 25 & 26, 2007
GREAT AMERICAN MUSIC HALL
W/ AZALIA SNAIL & CHARLIE PARR

SAN FRANCISCO MUSEUM of MODERN ART
PRESENTS COLLEGE NIGHT WITH NOISE POP
FEATURING REX RAY, PARADISE BOYS, AND JIMMY TAMBORELLO
SEPTEMBER 21, 2006
6 - 9PM

GOMEZ
AND
BEN KWELLER
MARCH 8 AND 9 | WEBSTER HALL
NYC

NOUVELLE VAGUE
FALL TOUR 2006

stellastarr*

NOISE POP AND ANOTHER PLANET ENTERTAINMENT PRESENT
TREASURE ISLAND MUSIC FESTIVAL
MODEST MOUSE • SPOON • BUILT TO SPILL • THIEVERY CORPORATION • GOTAN PROJECT • M.I.A. • KINKY
DJ SHADOW & CUT CHEMIST • CLAP YOUR HANDS SAY YEAH • AU REVOIR SIMONE • ZION I • M.WARD
TWO GALLANTS • GHOSTLAND OBSERVATORY • FLOSSTRADAMUS • SEA WOLF • EARLIMART
DEVIL MAKES THREE • STREET TO NOWHERE • TRAINWRECK RIDERS • FILM SCHOOL
DENGUE FEVER • HONEYCUT • WEST INDIAN GIRL • MOCEAN WORKER • KID BEYOND
SEPTEMBER 15 & 16, 2007

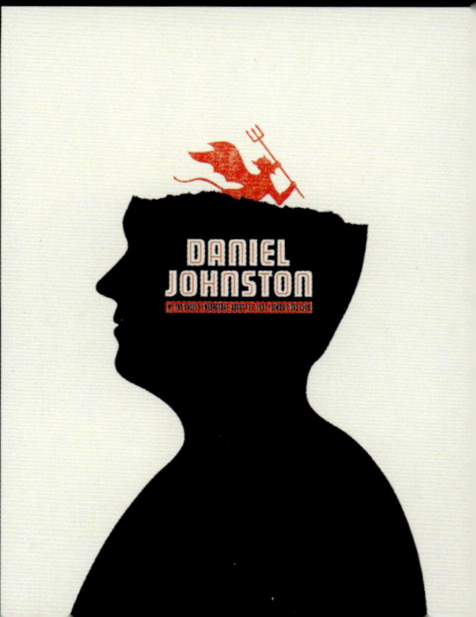

DANIEL
JOHNSTON

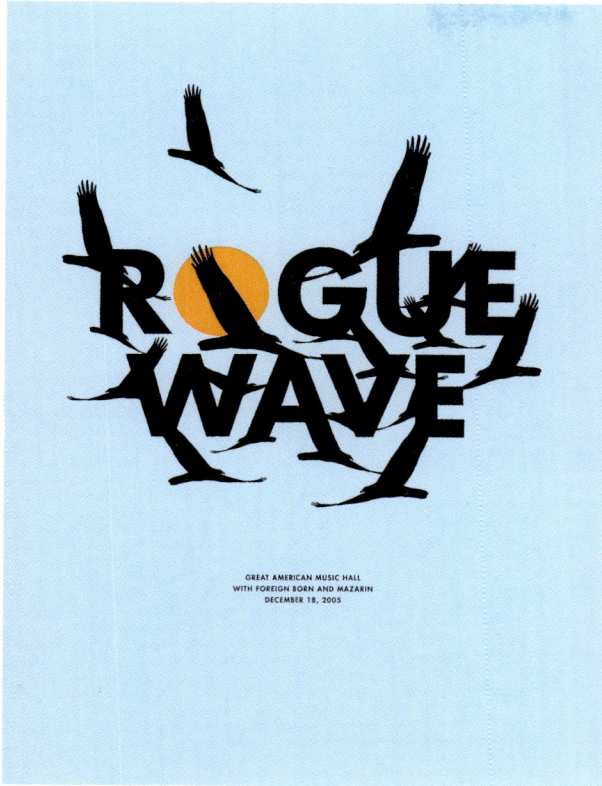

ROGUE WAVE

GREAT AMERICAN MUSIC HALL
WITH FOREIGN BORN AND MAZARIN
DECEMBER 18, 2005

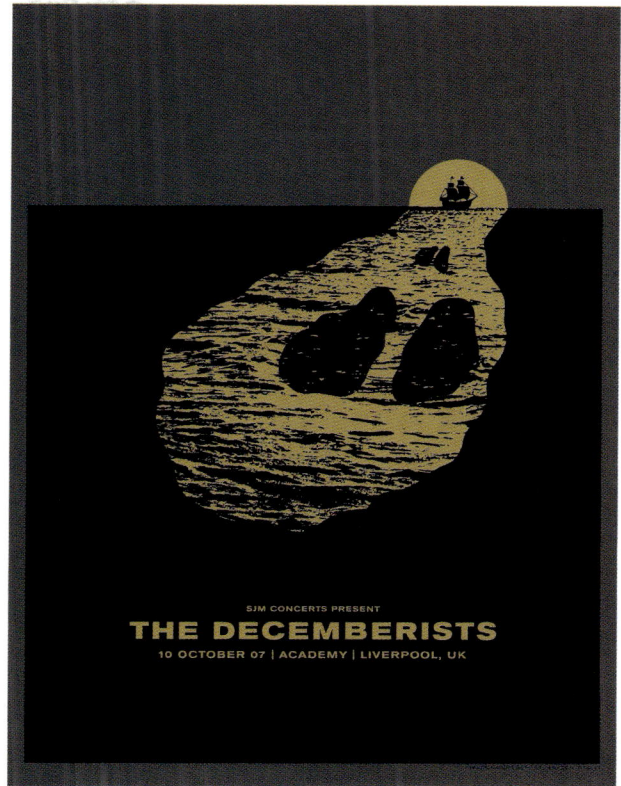

SJM CONCERTS PRESENT

THE DECEMBERISTS

10 OCTOBER 07 | ACADEMY | LIVERPOOL, UK

MODEST MOUSE

with MATT COSTA • TUESDAY, DECEMBER 11, 2007 • RIALTO THEATER • TUCSON, AZ

STARS

IN OUR BEDROOM AFTER THE WAR NOVEMBER 13 – 14, 2007

BIMBO'S 365 CLUB • SAN FRANCISCO, CA

PATENT PENDING

Patent Pending Industries is the design studio of Jeff Kleinsmith and Jesse LeDoux. "Working on CD packages and campaigns for a record label with someone is great, but posters are difficult," Kleinsmith says. "Having said that, I think that collaborating can be interesting if done right, and Jesse and I have done a bit of it. When we decide to collaborate, we try to do it in oddball ways. As just one example: Built To Spill played three nights in a row, so we did three posters, one for each night. We each did a night and had our printer mix up the films to make up the third night without showing us what he was going to do. Jesse and I didn't have a clue what each other's posters looked like, or what the printer did, until the prints came back."

LeDoux continues, "There has only been one poster, 'Vandermark 5,' where we took the traditional pass-back-and-forth method to collaboration. The others have been collaborations where we were able to continue working inside our respective bubbles. It isn't until the final step where we toss the results together to yield the final product. Whether it is designing the separations of a four-color poster independently from each other, collaborating on a common color palette alone, or one person does the type while the other does the image, our collaborative posters still have a heavy bipolar quality to them. They are really enjoyable, as it forces us to approach working together in very unconventional ways. We have similar design sensibilities and fully respect each other's work, yet when it comes down to the gritty details, we rarely arrive at the same answer. It probably explains why our posters compliment each other, while remaining glaringly obvious as to whether Jeff created it or me. Most often, we prefer to choose only one of us to work on any new poster job and see Patent Pending, the company, as the collaboration."

with **Earth**

TUESDAY, MAY 23, 2006 AT THE SHOWBOX THEATER
1426 1st Ave, Seattle, WA · 9pm All Ages · Advance tix from TicketsWest
Design by Jesse LeDoux (Patent Pending). Printed by Patent Pending Press.

SUPERSUCKERS
HOG MOLLY
THE CATHETERS
GRACELAND
FEB 16

WITH CALEXICO + WHY? JULY 2 SHOWBOX
$15.00 ADV AT TICKETSWEST AND ALL OUTLETS. $15.00 DAY OF SHOW AND AT THE DOOR. DOORS AT 9PM. ALL AGES.

DEATH CAB FOR CUTIE
NADA SURF / THE CATCH / SMOOSH

SHOWBOX NOVEMBER 21/22
Friday November 21st - The Showbox, Sonic Boom, Seattle Weekly and 90.3 KEXP presents DEATH CAB FOR CUTIE with NADA SURF and THE CATCH. Saturday November 22nd with NADA SURF and SMOOSH. $13.00 advance / $15.00 day of show at TicketsWest and outlets including Sonic Boom locations. Doors at 8PM. 21+. All ages doors at 6PM

THE SHINS

EASY STREET | FEB 20
QUEEN ANNE 20 MERCER ST | TUESDAY 12 NOON | LIVE!

Poster by Jesse LeDoux (Patent Pending).

JERMAINE ROGERS

Jermaine Rogers' distinctive line work and color use made him one of the most sought-after poster makers of the '90s. He has created nearly 800 music posters for performers such as Neil Young, Radiohead, Tool and David Bowie. More than just an advertisement for a show, Rogers' prints are often layered with meaning. In a poster for a Public Enemy show in Houston, Texas, fibrous roots connect a portrait of Chuck D to an illustration of Frederick Douglass.

His wide-eyed creatures—from soldier bunnies to a fanged teddy bear known as the Dero—are employed in satirical ways. A recent art print, "Respectfully Disagree," featuring a deranged raccoon wielding a dress shoe printed on top of a protest photo, comments on the incident in which an Iraqi reporter threw a shoe at President Bush. These singular characters have been transformed into a line of collectible vinyl toys.

His cartoony images feel as if they were ripped from the pages of a graphic novel, and he cites comic book artists as huge influences. He attributes his reliance on black and shadows to Graham Ingels, an EC Comics illustrator in the 1950s. Rogers' interests also include pulp fiction, ancient and esoteric texts, vintage toys and wax-museum figures.

"Aesthetically my biggest artist influence is Vincent van Gogh," Rogers writes on his website. "There aren't enough words for me to describe what the man's work and writings have done to inspire me. He's taught me to 'feel' art long before it falls out of my hands." Rogers also credits fellow poster maker Frank Kozik, who "not only showed me that it could be done, but how to do it."

A Houston native, Rogers now lives and works in Manitou Springs, Colorado, where he maintains a gallery space and studio called Dero 72. His current focus is on fine art and personal work.

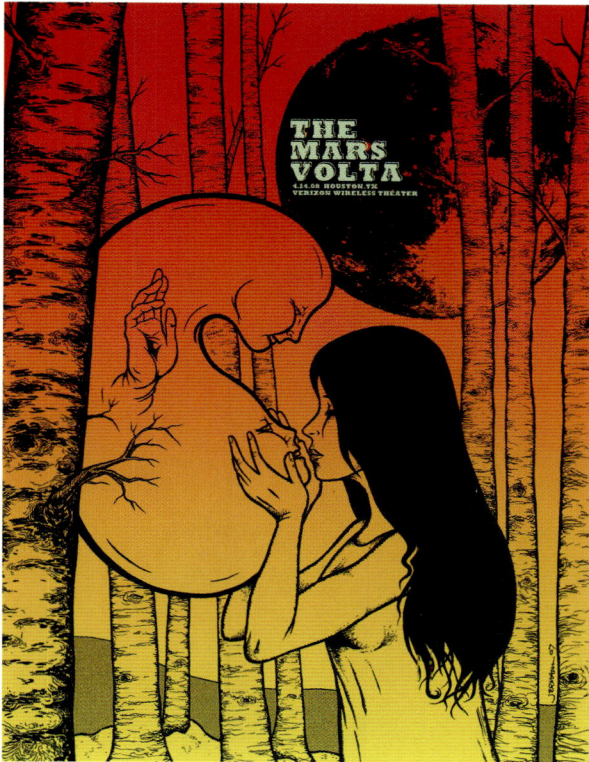

'You know I couldn't last....'
MORRISSEY
5.26.07 the backyard austin.tx ● 5.28.07 verizon wireless theater houston.tx
poster by jermaine rogers · 'supporting Moz since 1985'

'i will always exist. because i always exist.'
bauhaus
appearing at the sasquatch festival · live at the gorge
05·26·06
poster by j.rogers · www.jermainerogers.com

WEEN • FLAMINGLIPS • SONICYOUTH
W/THEMAGICNUMBERS SEPT.1ST N.Y.STATE FAIR
POSTER BY JERMAINE 2006   WWW.WEEN.COM   WWW.JERMAINEROGERS.COM

and every child walked out into the cold
night air... and surrendered thems

SIGUR·ROS
W/ AMINA
3·31·03 VERIZON WIRELESS THEATER

poster by JERMAINE 03   'at this point in his life, he had no hands...'

'TOMORROW BELONGS TO US.'

FANTOMAS
MELVINS BIG BAND
MAY 1 • THE FORUM • LONDON

'Turn me on, dead man'   www.jermainerogers.com

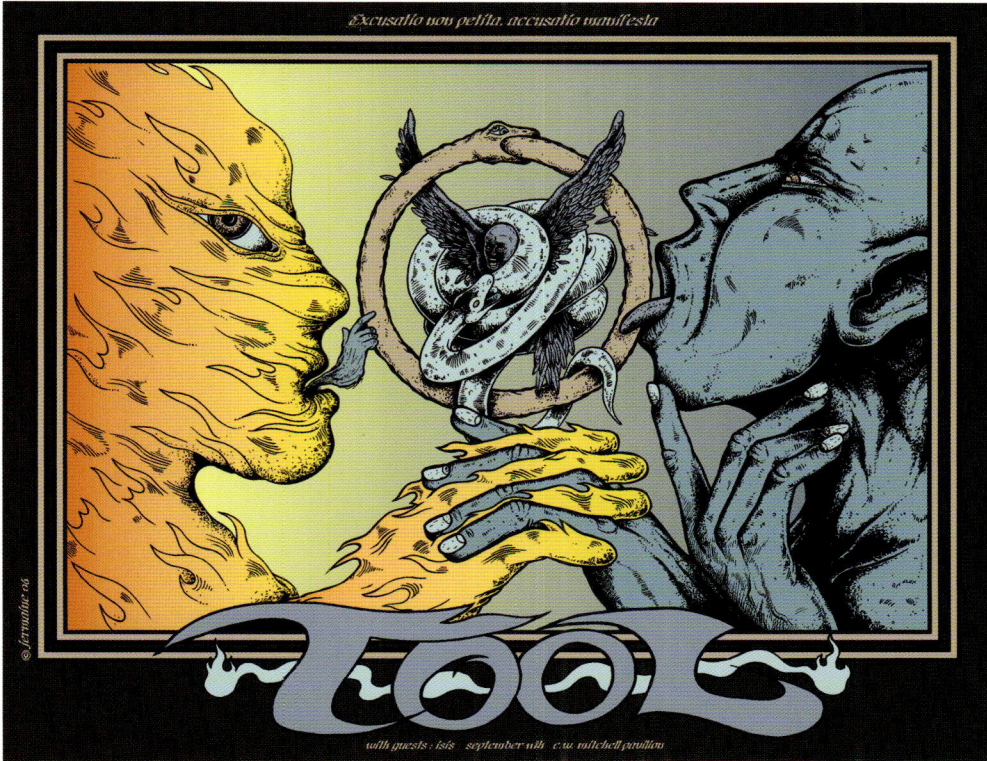

live nation presents...

SERIPOP

One look at the Seripop website reveals a printed output that staggers the mind. Based in Montreal, Chloe Lum and Yannick Desranleau started out making posters for bands, first their own and then their friends. Not long after, they had a ton of work on their hands.

On the subject of inspiration, Lum quickly reels off a list of her peers: Gunsho, Zeloot, Jelle Crama, Mat Daly, Keith Herzik, DNML, Greg Pizzoli, Mike DeForge and Jacinthe Loranger. She also mentions the Quebecois madman of poster design, Vittorio Fiorucci. "We're kind of inspired by everything around us—old signage, crappy graffiti, weird textile patterns, tile work, music, traveling, animals, wildlife," she explains.

The boundless energy these two possess spills over into the world of music as well. Their band, AIDS Wolf, is well known in avant/indie circles and tours in the states as well as Europe, releasing recordings on Skin Graft Records and Lovepump United. When the band tours, so does Seripop. "We'll just stay at the end of our band's tour and travel from city to city by train," Lum explains. "We try to concentrate more on creating work while on the road, collaborating and spending time with our friends in different cities." On a recent trip, they collaborated with Bongout on a poster in Berlin, had a drawing jam in Brussels, and made a "giant-assed" installation in Bremen.

Their lives, in many ways, are their art. "We're pretty much the authors of our own existence," Lum explains. "Most of the work we do is pretty free and personal. We do what we want, when we want to. We feel like we are leaving some type of mark—however dubious it may be—on popular culture, and that's pretty exciting. We travel the world playing music, making and showing our art. We're constantly meeting people who make inspiring stuff and live inspiring lives, and we feel lucky to sleep on their floors, collaborate and exchange ideas with them."

SEVERED SCREENPRINTER'S ARM

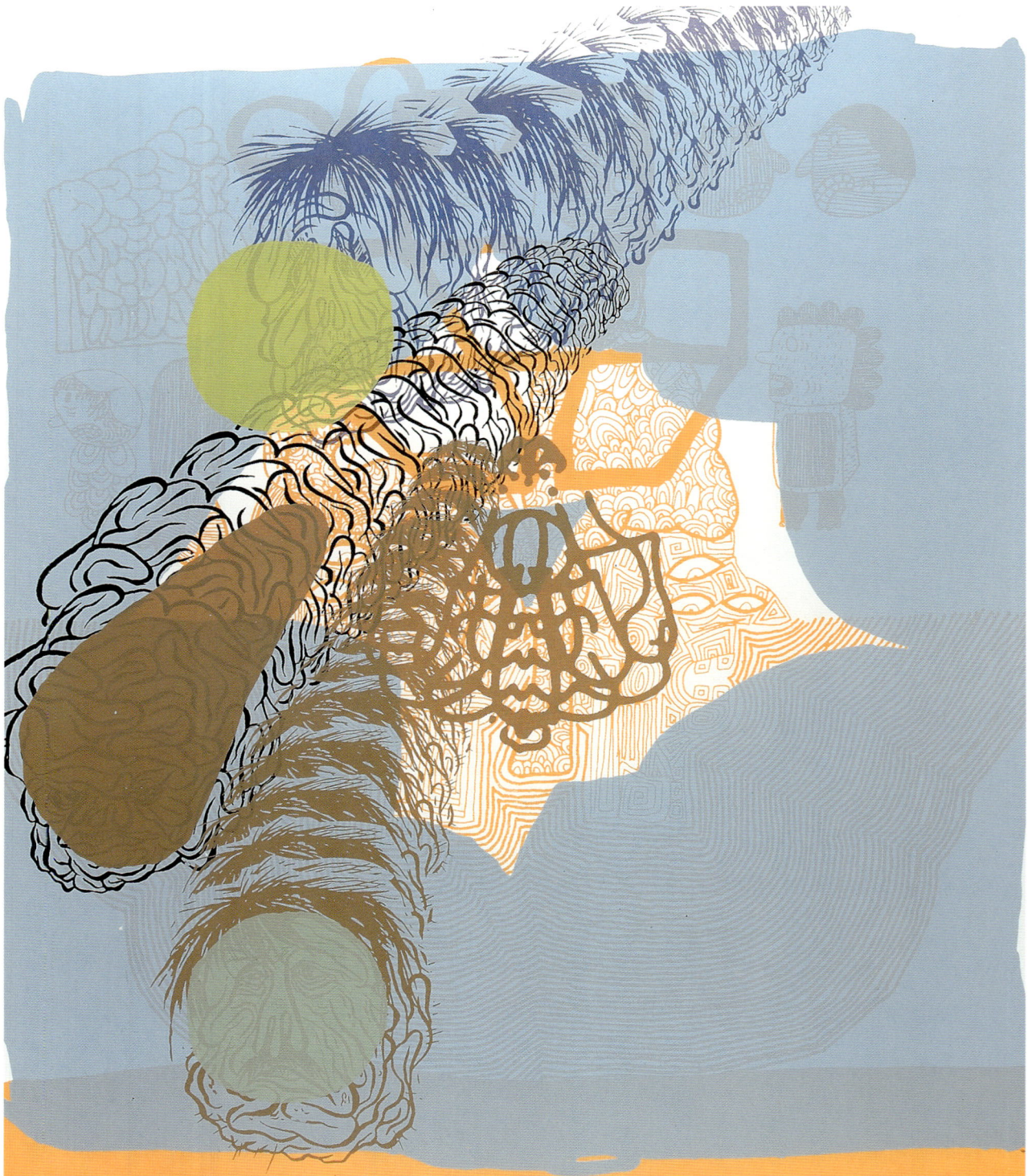

JANDEK SUNDAY JUNE 24 SALA ROSSA- 4848 St LAURENT
DOORS: 6PM SHOW: 7-9PM 18$AD/ 20$ DOOR PRESENTED BY
CORWOOD INDUSTRIES, SUONI PER IL POPOLO AND SIGNAL TO NOISE

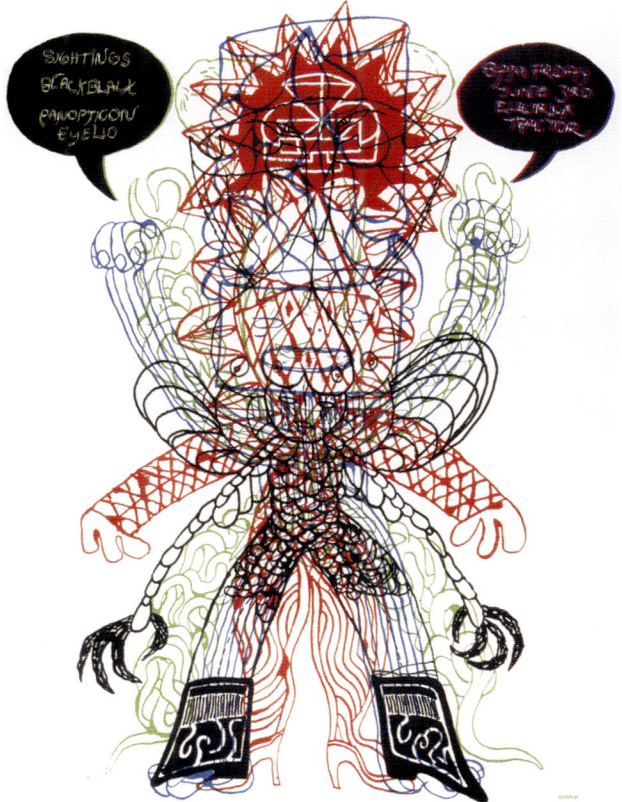

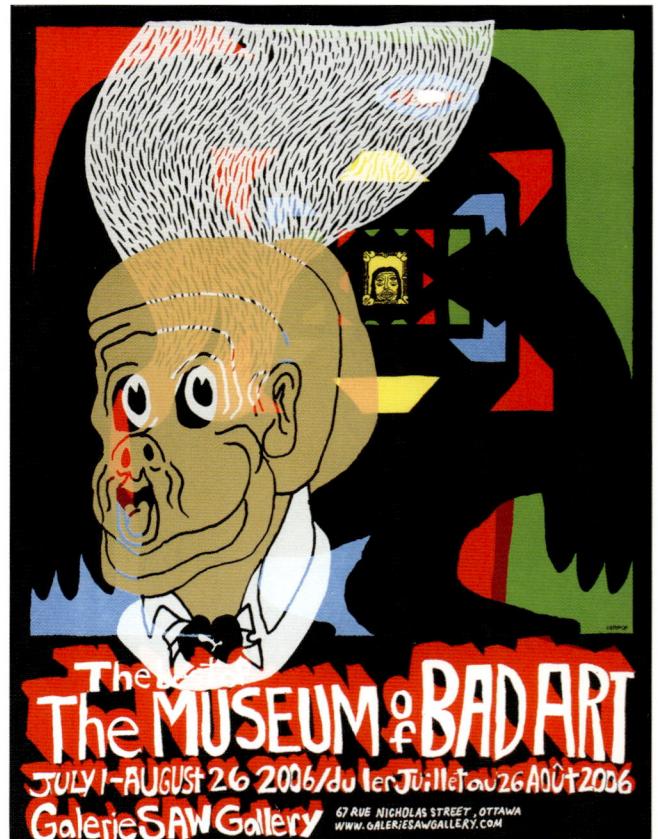

The MUSEUM of BAD ART
JULY 1 - AUGUST 26 2006/ du 1er Juillet au 26 Août 2006
Galerie SAW Gallery   67 RUE NICHOLAS STREET, OTTAWA
WWW.GALERIESAWGALLERY.COM

SONNENZIMMER

Nick Butcher and Nadine Nakanishi propel themselves into the world in a rush of painting, music, books and screenprinting. They bend shape and blend color to fit their individual visions and collective endeavors as Sonnenzimmer, which means "sun room" in German. While Sonnenzimmer is mostly a screenprinting operation, there is far more than that going on behind the door on the alley. That the door maintains its hinges, despite so much creativity busting out of the studio, stretches credulity. Veterans of the Bird Machine Operation in neighboring Skokie, these two have literally flown the coop to feather their own nest in the Roscoe Village section of Chicago.

It is difficult to put a label on what this couple is capable of doing. By one turn illustrative and another painterly, they carefully create dreamy, ghostly colorscapes that look like they could have been done in gouache, oil pastels or watercolors. Image shares the crown with negative space. Type is spartan, handdrawn and sometimes looks like it came from an old Letraset sheet. Abstraction takes place alongside the concrete and the fantastic. A certain kind of piquancy emerges that penetrates the thicket and provides a springboard for the viewer's mind to explore.

Both Nakanishi and Butcher find today's creative ferment to be exciting, but, as Butcher puts it, "Creativity and art-making are at a really interesting point. They are both exploding, in the sense that tons of people are making music, art, etc. But it's also extremely homogenized. It's awesome and frustrating all at once." For inspiration the two turn toward the natural and also look back to the era of the abstract expressionists, and movements like Bauhaus and Fluxus. Nakanishi is Swiss-Japanese, and she cultivates each influence in her art.

Music is a constant factor, especially for Butcher, who performs and releases his "homemade electronic music using cheap consumer goods." His first full-length work, *The Complicated Bicycle*, was released by Hometapes in 2005.

Now that Sonnenzimmer is a full-time operation, the couple finds themselves busier than ever. "It's been two years in the making, but we finally did it," Butcher says. "We are both so psyched to have made it to this point. When things slow down enough for us to realize what we are doing, we both freak out and laugh!"

The
Walkmen
with
Golem

FRIDAY, SEPTEMBER 12 / 2008
18 & OVER / 9PM

M METRO
3730 NORTH CLARK ST
CHICAGO

WEDNESDAY, SEPTEMBER 26
White Magic
Badawi
Holy Fuck
Burning Star Core with
Graveyards & Zac Davis
THURSDAY, SEPTEMBER 27
Pere Ubu
Ulrich Schnauss (Germany)
Hair Police
Glen Jones & Jack Rose
FRIDAY, SEPTEMBER 28
Gol
Excepter
Thomas Ankersmit (Netherlands)
Leslie Keffer
SATURDAY, SEPTEMBER 29
Deerhunter
Daniel Carter
No Age
Sin Ropas, with
the films of Brent Green
SUNDAY, SEPTEMBER 30
Boris (Japan)
Michio Kurihara (Japan)
Damon & Naomi
People
The Empty Bottle
ADVENTURES
IN MODERN MUSIC
SPECIAL EDITION

The Empty Bottle and the Wire present
Adventures in Modern Music
Agathe Max, Arnold Dreyblatt and his Orchestra of Excited Strings, Black Moth Super Rainbow, Blues Control, Busdriver, Colourmusic, Daedelus, Dead Machines, Ecstatic Sunshine, Evangelista, Flying Lotus, Henry Flynt, Icy Demons, Keiji Haino, Lau Nau, Musket, Paul Metzger, Shugo Tokumaru, These Are Powers, Tussle
Wednesday, September 10th – Sunday, September 14th, 2008

oRSo
with
Solow
ELECTRO/ACOUSTIC SERIES
Saturday,
December 2nd, 9pm
ELASTIC ARTS FOUNDATION 2830 N. MILWAUKEE AVE
ABOVE FRIENDSHIP CHINESE RESTAURANT

TILL BY TURNING
ERICA DICKER, VIOLIN | AMY CIMINI, VIOLA | SARAH BIBER, CELLO | KATHERINE YOUNG, BASSOON | EMILY MANZO, PIANO
PREMIERS MUSIC OF AARON SIEGEL AND SABRINA SCHROEDER | ALSO FEATURING WORKS BY CHRISTIAN WOLFF, HAROLD MELTZER, ALEXANDER NESS AND KATHERINE YOUNG | SATURDAY, MARCH 31, 2007 | 3PM | THE FRIEND'S SEMINARY MEETING HOUSE | 15 RUTHERFORD PLACE [BETWEEN 15-16TH STREETS | RUTHERFORD PLACE IS BETWEEN 2-3RD AVENUES] | $10 ADMISSION | WWW.TILLBYTURNING.COM

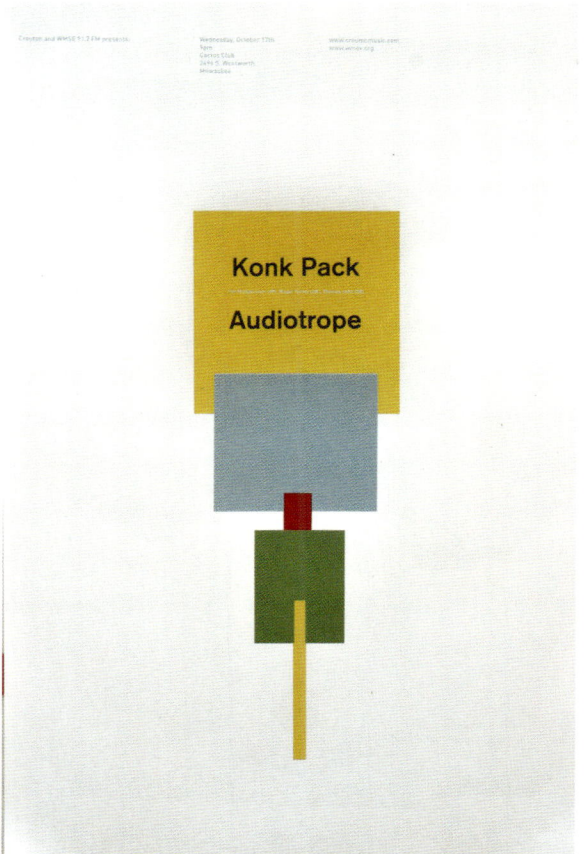

TYLER STOUT

Tyler Stout's posters are densely layered with iconic imagery, pulling at the eyes, tugging at the sleeve and sending the mind into orbit. As the layers of the composition unravel, discover familiar favorites and delight in new juxtapositions. Monsters, flowers, detritus, skulls, flags, bicycles, Datsuns and De Tomasos grow like vines in the heath of Stout's imagination.

Stout especially enjoys making posters because they afford him the "opportunity to experiment with styles and ideas," and finds inspiration in comic books, video games and movies. "I watch tons of movies while I work, mostly older ones I've seen many times," he says. "I find movies easier to listen to than music while I work, actually." His work often re-interprets classic movie posters or employs film imagery. "It's fun dealing with iconic characters like Jack Burton from *Big Trouble in Little China* or MacReady from *The Thing*," he says. "I enjoy these movies so much that having the opportunity to incorporate them into something I'm working on is pretty enjoyable." In one poster for the Alamo Drafthouse, a cinema in Austin, Stout incorporated countless characters—from Edward Scissorhands to Foxy Brown and beyond.

Like most kids, Stout started drawing at an early age. "I just didn't lose interest in it as I grew older," he says. Stout took art classes in high school and college and, after living in his parents' basement for a year, found a job at Vermont-based design studio JDK, where he did graphics for companies such as Burton Snowboards and Nike. "And from there it was all downhill," he says, jokingly. Today, Stout has worked for Puma, *Esquire*, Adidas and the Austin Film Society, among others. "Sometimes I'm able to do what people want," he says, "and sometimes it all ends in tears." He currently lives in Brush Prairie, Washington, with his wife, two children and three dogs.

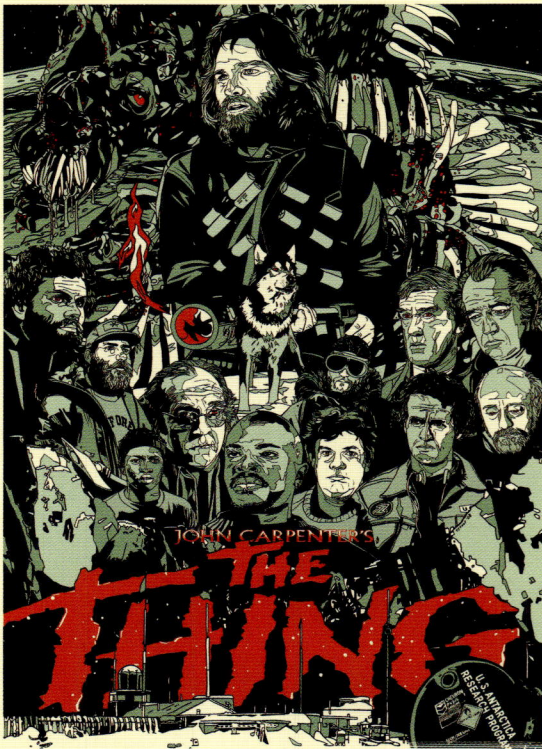

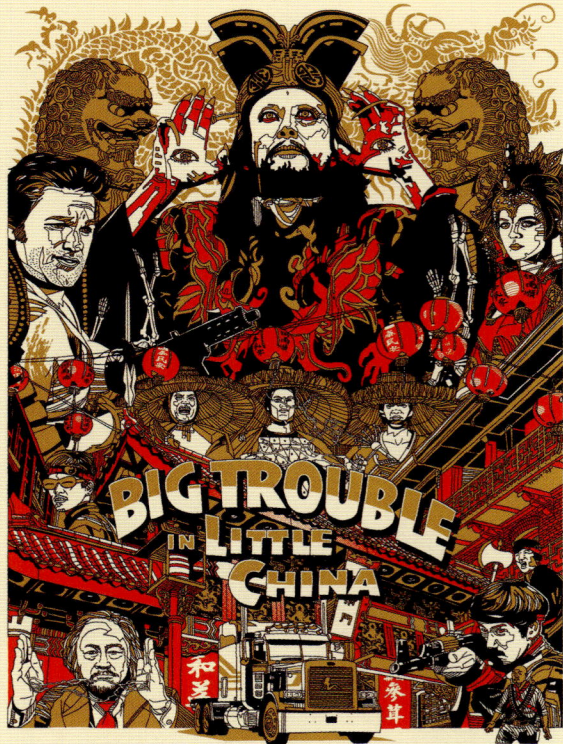

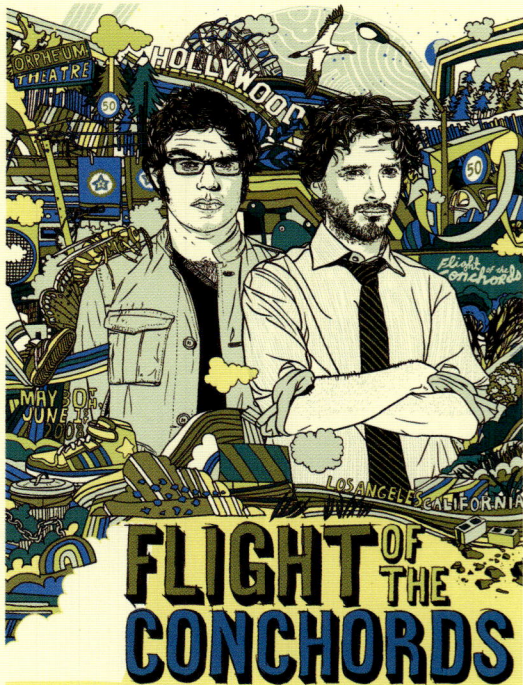

'THE WARRIORS' SCREENING AT CONEY ISLAND, NEW YORK, NY SHOWING ON AUGUST 2ND
2006 NETFLIX ROLLING ROADSHOW / WWW.NETFLIX.COM/ROADSHOW
MOVIE STARTS AT DUSK / PRODUCED BY ALAMO DRAFTHOUSE CINEMA

R RESTRICTED
Under 17 Requires Accompanying
Parent or Adult Guardian

POSTER BY TSTOUT | PRINTING BY D&L SCREENPRINTING   MADE IN U.S.A.

VERMONT INTERNATIONAL FILM FESTIVAL

October 11 - 14 • 2007

POLICE

BURLINGTON, VT - WATERFRONT THEATER / MERRILL'S ROXY CINEMA / FIREHOUSE CENTER

THINKMULE

In Jeremy Pruitt's art, lines aggregate to form creatures on textured fields of earthen color, bringing to mind a crazed, contemporary Lascaux. "I think it is just the response of me to nature and all the patterns in nature," he says. Pruitt has a free-flowing style that somehow gets reined in enough to be captured and fixed on paper. Images are cut up like a butcher's meat chart or X-rayed to show off maniacal, intestinal inner workings.

Frequently, markers of date and place find themselves in Pruitt's fine art print work. "I love history, and I have always loved buying photos in antique stores or at estate sales," Pruitt explains. "I really like to buy up whole lots of albums or pictures, that way I can see the whole progress of a person's life. This is how this came into my art: this idea of a sense of history, or that the image is capturing a moment in time."

The permeation of nature recurs in Pruitt's work, as flora and fauna inspire him. "I love to draw and watch birds," says Pruitt, who lives in Colorado. "Plants have been a big inspiration to me ever since I saw the work of Ernst Haeckle. His work is so beautiful."

To achieve his results, Pruitt starts with pencil drawings on paper. These in turn are scanned and composited on the computer. Sometimes he draws the entire piece at once, but more frequently works in parts, giving his work the room to grow naturally.

Pruitt started THINKMULE, his art and design site, 10 years ago. "It is my ideas, my passion, my contribution to the art world," he says. "I hope I can create something that people like, enjoy it myself and inspire someone else to create art."

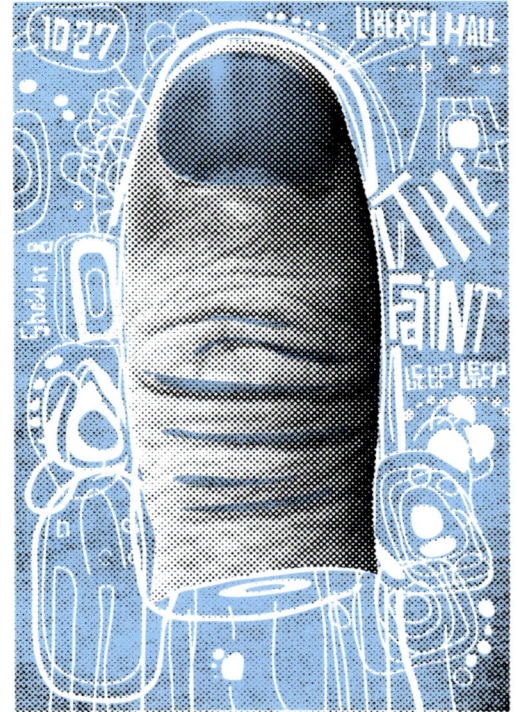

TORTOISE

W/BEANS   FREE ALL BEATS   SAT. JUNE 12   GRANADA THEATER   LAWRENCE KS   ALL AGES - 8PM

BEN WOODWARD

Ben Woodward begins his prints and paintings by drawing in front of the television or listening to the radio, and describes his aesthetic as "surrealism for people taught to read by Muppets." In his work, Woodward employs a unique cast of creatures capable of displaying a full range of human emotions. By using these humanoid characters that lack gender or race, Woodward hopes that the viewer will concentrate solely on the emotions and experiences being portrayed.

Woodward's goal is to "unite people in their common experience," which he does amazingly with his characters. Death, escapism, curiosity, community, shame, sharing, pride, self-loathing, self-love, introspection, generosity, communing with nature and friendship are just some of the emotions that come through in the vivid colors of Woodward's palette. The difficult-to-describe feeling of being unable to show or receive love is depicted in Woodward's paintings and prints. All of this occurs in Woodward's art despite a modest claim that "sleepy and reluctant acceptance" is the emotion that translates best for him.

Woodward was born in West Philadelphia in 1974 and, by his own admission, was "really bad at school." His dyslexia made reading and writing difficult, and this made him "draw all the time." During his teen years, his family moved to the suburbs, where he met Andrew Jeffrey Wright and Adam Wallacavage. These skate punks banded together to Xerox zines, print shirts and make art. The friendship and collaboration ultimately resulted in the formation of the now legendary Space 1026, a gallery and studio complex in Philadelphia. Woodward has illustrated a children's book called *Sullivan's Solo*, published by Free News Projects, and lives in Philadelphia with his wife Chi-eun Kim and their daughter Atari.

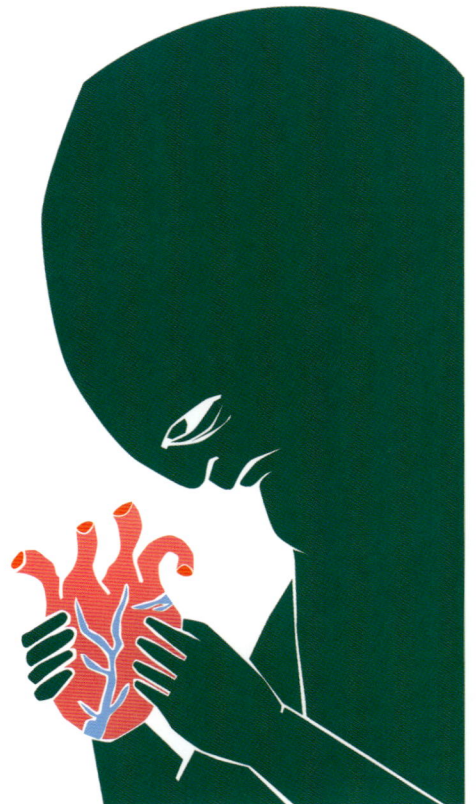

ANDREW JEFFREY WRIGHT

Andrew Jeffrey Wright grew up in the Philadelphia suburb of Ridley Township, a typical East Coast scene complete with lawns, Little League and backyard birthday parties. As a teenager in the 1980s, Wright skated the streets of his neighborhood, and it was through skateboarding that he met Adam Wallacavage. Wright discovered screenprinting in the basement of Adam's family home and, bitten by the bug, began printing shirts for his zine *The Underground Skate Mag*.

While earning his BFA in animation, Wright also took printmaking courses in college, and the process captivated him. "For making multiples or one-of-a-kind rare prints, screenprinting is the process I love most," he says. "I enjoy the physical action of pulling a squeegee and watching the print develop layer by layer. It's like watching Jesus being born."

A streak of irreverent humor runs throughout Wright's work. Behind the neon colors and playful imagery, there is often a message exposing capitalist greed, or one that brings beauty to light. The fact that we live in what Wright calls a "Jekyll and Hyde society" explains his seemingly divergent messages.

Repetition and abstract designs are prevalent in much of Wright's work, sometimes invoking American quilt making. In one piece titled "41,000 Faces," Wright creates a psychedelic interlocking pattern that shows the interconnectedness of humanity. In other works, the repetition produces an optical illusion that the prints are moving. To make these patterns, Wright uses silkscreening, cassette tapes, collage and paint. He says an "uncontrollable urge" drives him to work on his art eight to 10 hours a day.

Wright lives, works and rides his bicycle like a maniac in the city of Philadelphia. He is a founding member of the Space 1026 collective to which he attributes the fact that he makes so many screenprints.

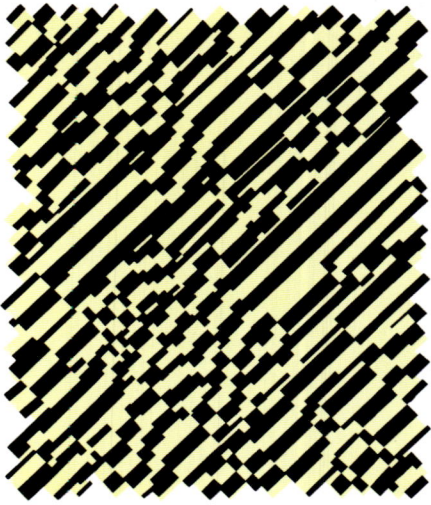
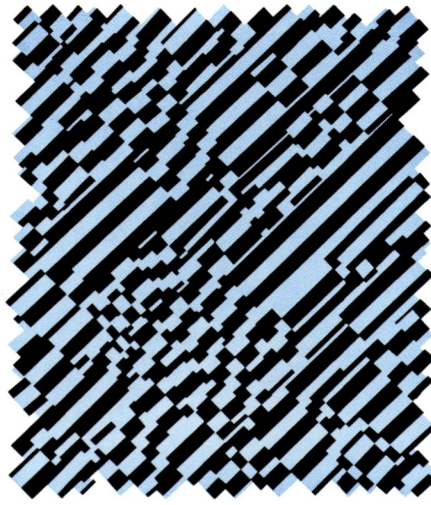
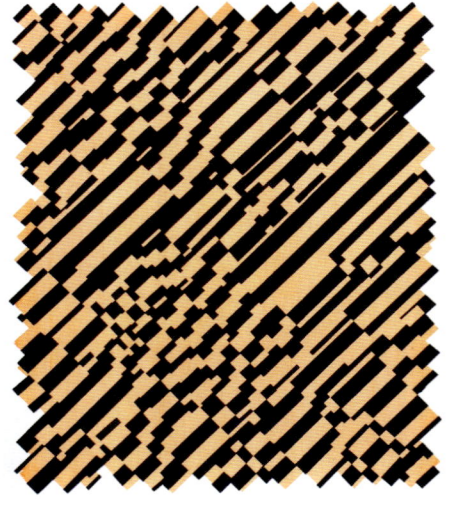

PEE comics
by Crystal and Andrew J. Liu.

uh oh —

ARTIST INDEX

Image by Michael Motorcycle

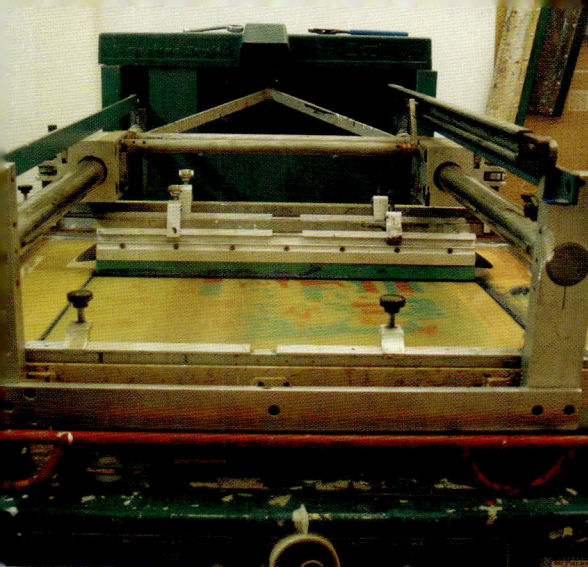

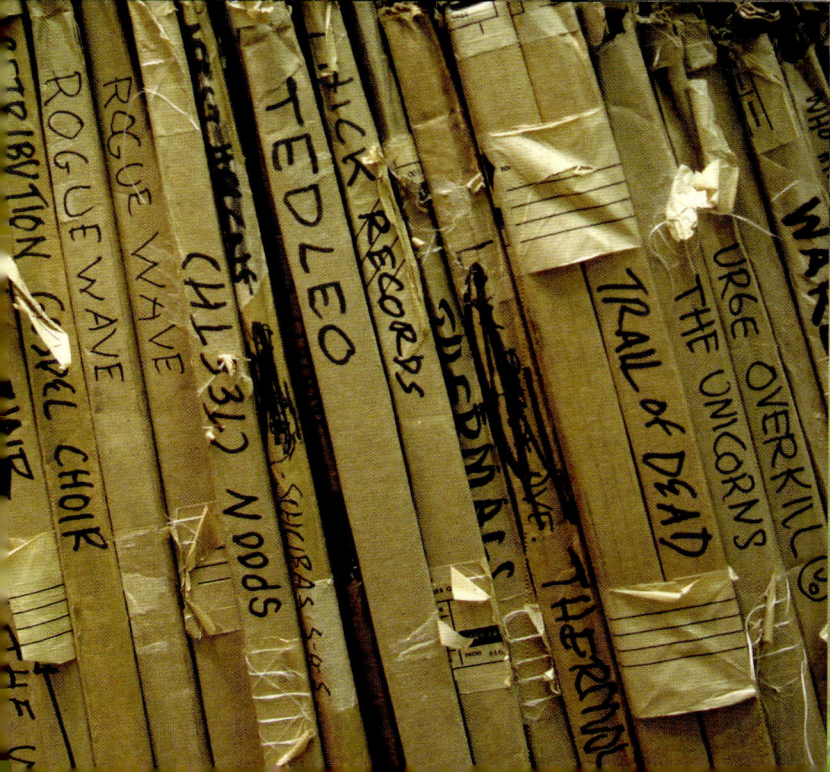

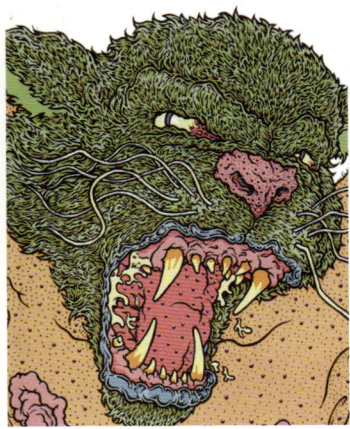

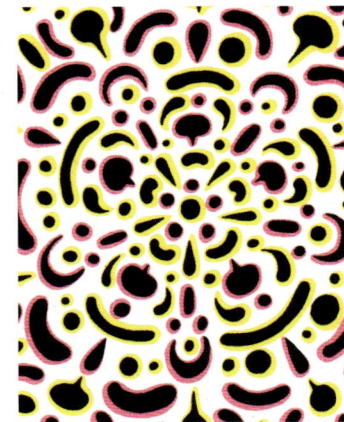

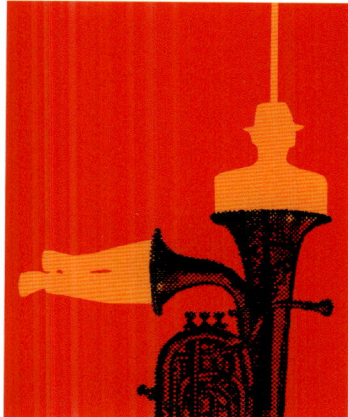

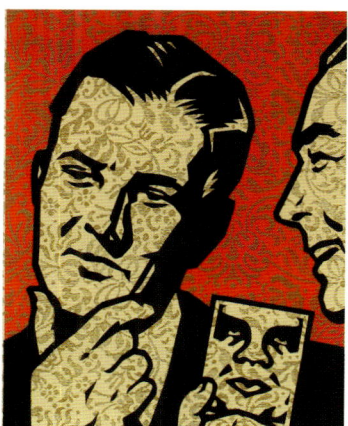